THE SPLIT-LEVEL
FELLOWSHIP

THE
SPLIT-LEVEL
FELLOWSHIP

By
WESLEY C. BAKER

PHILADELPHIA

THE WESTMINSTER PRESS

PUBLISHED BY THE WESTMINSTER PRESS®

PHILADELPHIA, PENNSYLVANIA

PRINTED IN THE UNITED STATES OF AMERICA

To Evelyn, my mother, who introduced me to a church whose life can receive questions and bear discussion, and

To the memory of William, my father, who left a goodly heritage of layman's observations, descriptive quips, rich humor, and a full measure of faithful personal integrity

CONTENTS

THE SPLIT-LEVEL
FELLOWSHIP

PREFACE

The complaining wartime draftee mumbled about his gruff sergeant, "He wasn't born, he was issued!" Likewise, this book wasn't born in the conventional manner; it *emerged*, from the fabric of a ministry. It oozed, involuntarily, through the pores of organic tissue surrounding the living concepts encountered in the pulpit. Remarks, impressions, hunches, notes, speeches, class lectures, midnight reveries, all seemed to accumulate unity and momentum until there was no way of preventing this outpouring of ideas. No claim can be laid to originality— the propositions appearing here simply fell out of the sky, in conversation, in research, in life in the church.

It was Dr. Robert Lee, Professor of Christian Social Ethics at the San Francisco Theological Seminary, who made the request that congealed the mass of concepts into form; he invited me to be one of the speakers in the Institute of Ethics and Society at San Anselmo in the spring of 1963. I wrote the lecture, and found myself hopelessly carried away. Most of that lecture is here, scattered throughout the work with Dr. Lee's permission. The same lecture was given over station KXKX-FM, San Francisco, in September, 1963.

Dr. David Eitzen, of the Southern California School of Theology, gave thoughtful guidance on Chapter V, as did Dr. Franklin Littell, of the University of Chicago, on Chapter II, and Dr. Randolph Crump Miller, of Yale Divinity School, on Chapter VII. The friendly counsel of Dr. Roy Fairchild and Dr. John R. Bodo, of San Anselmo, is felt throughout. A portion of Chapter VIII appeared in 1954 in the little magazine *Prophetic Realism*, edited by Dr. John Wick Bowman. My loyal secretary, grammarian, and style critic, Wilma R. Grant, did all the hard manuscript work, rendering herself completely indispensable and the recipient of my gratitude and devotion.

To whom is this book directed? Officers in local congregations, church school teachers, college professors, and denominational executives make up a corporate heterogeneous hoped-for target. I also have in mind that large host of fellow ministers who are groping for clearer assurances about the ministry and the relevance of the church. It is designed to be usable in lay study groups, leadership training, youth institutes, campus conversations, and women's circles. And, although it speaks the language of those who carry the burdens of the church, it is possible that "outsiders" (whoever *they* may be) could find some entertainment value, even a wee bit of learning, in shooting down the trial balloons herein launched.

Thank heavens, I do not and cannot speak ex cathedra; these are ideas that need circulation, discussion, modification, and correction. The sooner this book becomes obsolete, or "old hat," the better. It is intended to be a springboard into reality thinking about the church, and should create further developments. These will, hopefully, come from all kinds of people dealing with the subject matter responsibly. To this end I solicit answering cannonades from all quarters, and entrust the ensuing conversation to the Lord of the church.

W. C. B.

San Rafael, California

INTRODUCTION

The view from the pulpit is a privileged sight. Those of us who have access to it, professionals and the small cadre of courageous laymen, are considerably divided as to just what we really see. All of us approach the holy desk with preconceived images of what the view will be like, some over-romantic, others cynical. In retrospect, I must admit to beginning my ministry with rather unfounded elements of both.

And what a view it is! The pious at prayer, the curious alert but guarded, the bored nearly asleep, and the troubled on the verge of tears are always there. They come by habit, by conscience, by virtue of a whole host of nonreligious, even antireligious, reasons . . . from fear, from guilt, from loneliness, and to modify the cruelty of reality. He who ministers in their midst can expect to be exalted, admired, tolerated, manipulated, detested, feared, and used. This is a weekly experience for me; it has left its high-water and its drainage marks. It has lifted me to exuberance and left me chastened and broken.

But it is not so much the Sunday-by-Sunday view about which I write here. One learns little from cafeterialike visits in even the strongest churches of the land. I would rather relate here the observations that come from a *cumulative* view, the collection of years of face-to-face confrontation, watching the pilgrimage of people, families, clans, communities, entering, praying, offering up their problems, relating in timidity or temerity with one another. One can't watch expectancy wane into disappointment, eagerness into ennui, and good intentions fade quietly without feeling that some things could be constructively said about the church.

The view, of course, sees through and beyond the Sunday-best, the formal worship. As the hymns are sung and the prayers endured, clerical eyes scan the congregation, knowing with sadness that the outside life is not as visibly excited about the gospel as seems here. Even in the colorful pageantry of Sunday morning, thoughts occur to the preacher of these same people elsewhere at other times; he sees them in his mind's eye as he smiles at them from the chancel.

The twentieth century is full of many mysteries. As the strictly defined areas of life drop away, and differences between rich and poor, ruler and subject, authority and dependence, become vaguer, something of agonizing indefiniteness enters into common experience and becomes expressed in a scramble for assurance. Try as we might to drown out the voice of inquiry by turning up the volume of the superficial—the greater horsepower, the increased square footage, the extra bathroom, and the deeper water-ski tan—we still feel the mystery and face our lonely hours with dread.

It is not so much a mystery of What can I do to meet the situation? but For heaven's sake, what *is* the situation? The uncertainty is not how life functions, but what, in the long run, life *is*, anyway. The golden culture of Western man has set a beautiful and well-equipped stage for history's most gripping drama—but somehow has forgotten to identify the cast. And so the classic mystery prevails that previous generations only toyed with academically: What is man?

The acuteness of this painful vacuum is evident in all portions of American life. As skillfully conceived commercials contrive to make men into dutifully obedient statistics—as mores attempt to make us morally neutral—just so do the brassy supermarket and gleeful society columnist cry out to us of the mystery. The family circle, now gathered round the TV or the neighbor's swimming pool, succeeds when it echoes the language of the time, and writhes in discomfort if it ever discovers an unmodern or creative tendency.

But of all places in Western civilization where the clash and the cry of man against his own mystery are the loudest, the chief is the local parish church. Outwardly innocuous, and apparently culturally captive, the corner congregation is undeniably caught in an unresolvable conflict, constantly drawing a small handful of innocents into the fiery furnaces of facing the mystery without anesthetic, and spewing out into the unsuspecting world a small host of disciplined maturity.

The well-supported conspiracy of modern times to defuse

the church and make it, rightly, a captive and controllable way station of culture has not quite succeeded—yet. Not that there was any conscious opposition to the conspiracy—just inner voices that could never be stilled. For of all the arenas of the human drama, the church has always been involuntarily committed to be the battlefield between the Temporary Evidence and the Essentially True. Down deep, every man knows that this *must* be a conflict supreme; he both senses and dreads that he cannot avoid this clash, and that at its most exotic truth-bringing it is accompanied by excruciating agony.

It is this which makes most men flee from the church, but in that very flight there is a furtive confession of belief, tossed backward over the shoulder in rejective fear—like the cry of the demon: "What have you to do with me, Jesus, Son of the Most High God? I adjure you by God, *do not torment me*" (Mark 5:7). Strangely enough, it is this very fear that has added to the church's prestige among the fearful. This tacit acknowledgment of validity and relevance affirms the continuing battle of Armageddon that goes on in every parish.

It is most terrible, this head-on clash, for both forces are brutally strong, and represented profoundly well in the church. The prominent and apparently stronger side is that of the today—the here and now. Basically, it is the call from beneath to use society, culture, money, and the church, to become instruments of the finite motive. Most especially, use the church. Make it to be a manipulatable assurance within time that man has eternity under control and that the mystery has an easy answer. How desperate we are for this to be possible! No one, including the mightiest bishop and selfless saint, has ever been more than arm's reach from this desperation, and those who have felt it the strongest were the more aware of its dismal devastation. If only there were a usable formula, an available capsule, to dissipate the mystery! We *must* find it, and the church must express it, lest we be plunged into the torment of an endless personal pilgrimage. God forbid!

In the parish church, this temporal side never completely wins. True, it appears to prevail, sometimes for generations. Many congregations have safely inane leadership and carefully circumscribed programs, with definite intention not to offend, but the struggle is only driven underground, where in unspoken silence the exploration continues, and companies pass one another in the spiritual catacombs, searching like Nicodemus under the cover of darkness. And, occasionally, throughout Christendom there are those centers where the battle breaks out on the surface, usually distressing and disturbing all touched. In the melee of this chaos, in the throes of this pain, the gospel, in fragmented splendor, appears briefly with healing in its wings, and the church remains alive. That it does so remains the great unexplained miracle of all time, and those of us who continue to be hurt and healed within the church bear the awful responsibility of serving within it with constantly reforming loyalty.

Frankly, it isn't easy. The same contradictions that trouble the spiritual neophyte rise to gargantuan proportions to those who lead, and the elementary task of conjuring up an adequate image of the church is a full-time pursuit. It is to accomplish this, and to offer a hopefully clarifying definition of the church with the use of "factor Beta," that this work is offered. As a starting foothold, no better contemporary source can be found than Karl Barth himself.

Remarking that the church is a summons, a call to the chosen community that is set apart by the grace of God to its full "chosenness," Dr. Barth uses the familiar words of the Nicene Creed.

The church, he says, is one. The visible and the invisible church are one and the same. Its essential unity arises out of its fidelity to its purpose.

The church is holy, in that it belongs to God, and not to man. Worst of all idolatries is the manipulation of the church to reflect the projected ideals of man. The holy church is only church when it belongs without reservation to God.

The church, continues Dr. Barth, is catholic, which means that it is universally true, based not on numbers, but only on the actual superiority of truth. "Catholicity," he writes, "means literally universality, not a numerical majority."

The church is apostolic, in that it is vested with delegated power which means divine responsibility. It is this word "apostolic" which will flavor much of the thinking in this book, for it enforces upon the church a nature conflicting with the secular concepts of the day. The apostolic church exercises its apostolicity in sheer obedience to its nature. It is what I call the "oboe-ness" of the church. A symphony orchestra, to produce a balanced tone, will need a sea of violins and a supporting plurality of cellos, violas, string basses, cluster groups of trumpets, horns, and percussion. But it needs only one or two oboes; the pungent, nasal, piercing, commanding cry of the oboe is utterly unique and unblending. Yet it is a leading voice that gives integrity and fullness to the whole orchestra. Its call is to be the oboe, not to assume the richer tones of the violins or clarinets, but to remain stubbornly and uniquely itself, that all other voices may know themselves the more clearly in contrast. Whenever any oboist, threatened by his loneliness or unusualness, blends his tone, he has forgone his own oboe-ness. This is, if you please, the apostolicity of the oboe, to speak faithfully to its own nature. The church is apostolic. The apostolicity of the church, the oboe-ness, is not so much a manipulated afterthought as it is an honest allegiance to its real nature.

And, Barth concludes, the church is believing. It both believes *in* the church and believes *the* church.

It's really quite a view that we have, we professionals, we leaders, we propagators of the history, custom, tradition. Some of us are as forthright as the Bishop of Woolwich, John Robinson, whose treatise *Honest to God* (The Westminster Press, 1963), however correct it may be, is a call to theological courage. Most of us are somewhat reluctant to be caught in creative controversy. But all of us to some measure understand Jeremiah's complaint that "there is in my heart as it were a burning fire shut up in my bones, and I am weary with holding it in, *and I cannot*" (Jer. 20:9b). The view that I have from the pulpit sees the reality of a split-level church, two different, but mutually valuable, parts of the Christian family. I call this view "factor Beta."

To the question, What is the purpose of the church? these answers were given by officers in a suburban Los Angeles parish:

> *"To train my children the difference between right and wrong."*
>
> *"To protect our country from Communism."*
>
> *"To make me feel better."*
>
> *"To teach my children the Bible."*
>
> *"To help people relax and enjoy each other."*
>
> *"To keep the community reminded of its duties."*
>
> *"To keep our kids off the street."*
>
> *"To preach Christ only—and to keep out of politics."*
>
> *"To help me out of trouble."*
>
> *"To make sick people well."*
>
> *"To do God's will."*

I

WHO SETS THE PACE?

There seems to be some confusion in the popular ideas of the church as to whether it should direct or be directed. The majority of observers, both Christian and otherwise, see the church as a phenomenon of history through which man expresses his noble nature, and therefore its best service is to be what the best of men want it to be. As a consequence, even with those who function in church leadership, life values tend to be expressed in nonreligious terms.

Two doctors work side by side in a California hospital for five years before discovering that they are both elders in neighboring Presbyterian churches. ("Why? What difference would it have made?") High school students responding to a survey see no connection between church affiliation and standards of vocational choice. White Citizens Councils throughout the Southern United States are usually predominantly manned by active Protestant Christians. Church members who visit deprived sections of the world frequently return in scorn. Commercial and foreign policies are usually developed out of institutional expediency with some humanitarian values added as salt and pepper. Negroes seeking racial justice are forced to voice dismay over the ineffectiveness of the church, from Martin Luther King's deeply loyal disappointment to the extreme hostility of the Black Muslim.

Beloved folklore tells us that Lord Nelson put the telescope to his blind eye at the moment of crisis, thereby winning the day. Many of us contemporary Christians have the uneasy feeling that the church is trying to perpetuate Trafalgar and prefers the nonsight of the blind eye to the painful insight of learning the truth. Like the person who fears cancer and prefers the worry to the facts, we find the most comfortable ecclesiastical posture to be the head in the sand, with the posterior plumes aloft. Herewith is a plea for critical, loyal objectivity within the ranks.

Everybody realizes that the church ought to be a disciplined community. Most everybody knows that it is not, especially in the Protestant sector. Franklin Littell, pleading the restoration of Methodism in a *Christian Century* article, sees the whole matter rotating around the "Discipline" being taken seriously. Presbyterian procedures carefully define, in frightening detail, the manner of local "quality control" by the church session, and the nearly universal disuse of these paragraphs is thunderous. Even the traditional communicants preparation classes and confirmation standards of the classic denominations have become more intake rituals than filtering-out processes, and should in all honesty be recognized as such.

Everybody knows it. At least intuitively we sense that our vapid "dependence" on the Holy Spirit to bring strength to the church contains an overmeasure of flight from being awkwardly discriminatory and too responsibly authoritative. Further, we are somewhat uncertain as to how seriously we can press for significant discipleship without throwing the church to an institutional disadvantage—and our confusion is compounded by an inability to make clear choice between.

Everybody knows it, and like Mark Twain's weather, there seems to be little that anyone can do about it. After all, the church is a fact of history and a contemporary given: few Christians outside of the radical fringe really deeply feel that the church can ever come up with new answers. Indeed, it doesn't have to; the old ones will do all right if they can only be revived.

Thereby hangs the tale. All the other aspects of man's common life have accelerated in pace. Whereas once it took centuries for a community to develop, and then decades, now full-grown cities can explode in weeks. Concepts and philosophies that formerly had the luxury of "cooking on the back burner" of speculation and experience now suffer the same fate as a popular song; instead of being filtered through generations of life and thought, major ideas now appear briefly on a hit parade, disappearing into obscurity before the college generation that loved them can graduate. But the church, the community of conviction and consolation, the corporation of concern, the incarnation of the inconceivable, cannot move that fast. Its rootage is still in those depths of mysterious existence to which the frenzied pace of modern living is alien.

This does not mean that the church is frozen in the glaciers of history, forced to grind along at minuscule speeds while life passes it up. Its basic references are always valid, wherever man is. But it does mean that she must be seen by the passing multitudes in her actual context, which may be far more contemporary than even the words we use.

There, we've even done it ourselves!

"She," we called the church. The sympathetic feminine, the perpetual mother who shelters us in our hurts, who warmly accepts us as we are, and who weeps over our failures, she is our all-inclusive community. *Qahal* and *ekklēsia*, the bride of Christ (II Cor. 11:2; Rev. 19:7), the subject of John XXIII's *Mater et Magistra*, no one would have the poor taste to ascribe masculinity to the communion of saints.

This may be a serious symbol confusion. The issue is not related to the actuality of male-female characteristics, whatever they may be, but the imagery and its appeal to widely held association. Femininity popularly connotes passivity, nonauthoritative guidance, a readiness always to reflect in softened tones whatever the prevailing values of the masculine world may direct. In requiring the motherly role of the church, the generations have made her to be submissive and obedient when the times called for the lonely but effective masculine cry of the prophet.

In his study of the Biblical imagery of the church, Paul

Minear points out[1] that the feminine reference was minimal in New Testament times; he relegates it to the category of minor images. Rather, he indicates that the major concepts of the church of the first century, such as "the people of God," "the new creation," "the fellowship in faith," are quite distant from the maternal. The most widely used picture in the epistles is "the body of Christ," making the gender rather obvious. It is, therefore, the settled reflection of the centuries that has emasculated the picture of the church's nature. As Minear comments, there is no "congeniality between the New Testament thought world and the contemporary Christian thought world."[2]

So deeply ingrained into the life and thought of the mind of today are the different sex roles and their apparent meanings in all aspects of daily life that this is an extraordinarily important point. Margaret Mead contends that the definition of maleness in America mainly comprises of "beating women in every game that both sexes play, in every activity in which both sexes engage."[3] The contrary definition of femaleness is that of always coming in second in all such activity. When Katherine Bliss contends that women have never been the makers of institutions, she sustains the current conceptuality.

Yet the New Testament reveals a church that entered into the life of the world with a definitely masculine—that is, directive leadership—intention. It attacked the passivity of the ancient world with its energetic and courageously innovative *kērygma*. The young church evidently had little intention of soothing the wounds, of giving sanctuary to the broken lives of its contemporary world; rather, it brought a new direction, a new pronouncement on the meaning of life and the richness of existence. The somewhat rugged and masculine aspect of forgiveness, in which a person squarely faced the unforgivable nature of his sins, seeing they could be forgiven, effected through God's grace enormous power for new life.

The mythological assumption that the church is feminine has through the years always forced it to be the figure of reflection and confirmation. Femininity never runs counter to the prevailing scale of values; rather, it always modifies it into acceptable terms. Masculinity accepts the demand of courageous nonconformity and introduces into the stream of history elements that dare to contradict and forcibly realign the values that are there. Certainly the lessons of the twentieth century obviate this psychology. In the Lateran Treaty of 1929, Benito Mussolini rather cleverly manipulated the Roman Catholic Church into a position of passivity, ingeniously preparing the way for the advance of fascism in Italy with the meek consent of ecclesiastical power. Hitler did not consider the church of Jesus Christ to be that much of a force to reckon with, but rather, assuming the directive and masculine role of leader and dictator, took careful advantage of the feminine aspect of the church, and simply became her lord and master. This he was able to do to the extent that the moral tone of a heretofore Christian culture could be so radically affected as to make room for the ghastly devastation of genocide.

Do we dare call the church "he"? Dare we to assume that the church has a masculine role in history, in community, in personal life? Would we ever rally to the picture of the gaunt, bearded prophet, giving his voice that cries in the wilderness, laden with judgment, provoking discipline, and proclaiming the Kingdom of God in basso profundo?

Whether we dare or not, the world prefers not to, and has recruited most Christians to agree. Because of the unspoken assumption that the church is called to obey the strongest voice and become its servant and spokesman, few there are who are courageous enough to claim otherwise. A survey was taken of the "power structure" of a small American college town, under the auspices of the Board of Christian Education of the Presbyterian Church U.S.A. in 1957. The writer was one of the dozen interrogators who interviewed the influential civic leaders to determine the center of decision-making for the town's corporate life. To the question of the effect of the church upon such matters, the answer seemed almost universally to be on the second level of the power pyramid. This means that the essential decisions were made without any connection with church teachings or organization, but that the expediting of these decisions was carried on by the churches among other civic groups, as ex post facto instruments of the decisions.

It would be wrong, of course, to make the church exclusively masculine. The twin functions of priest and prophet have the polar relationship of the genders, and the ministry of the church includes both. But just as all life will tend to wax sentimental over mother, and distantly respectful (or resentful) about father, so will the Christian community love its priestliness and rationalize its prophethood. We appreciate the term "pastoral care"; we recoil from Calvin's "churchly discipline." We praise the church when it upholds our values; we feel alienated and bitter when it dares to judge us.

In short, we prefer to keep the church feminine. This is a rough-and-tumble, dog-eat-dog, man's world. The church, we imply, would be embarrassed to know the real vulgarities of life; 'twere well, for her sake, she be protected from the harshness of reality and kept in her place. Even John Calvin stated that the church is mother of all who have God for their father.

And what is to happen to a community that remains distinctly and perpetually feminine? To seek out a roughly comparable relationship among the historic nations of the earth, behold the two ancient cultures of China and Japan. If there ever has been any unity attributable to Chinese culture, it would probably have to come under the heading of "being feminine." Passive, receptive, indulgent, productive, and absorbent, China has accepted most of its unique values from elsewhere. Confucianism, Taoism, are not so much positive affirmations of the meaning of life as they are indulgent rationalisms about the life that is already there. Buddhism, the dominant religion, is borrowed from India, and has gained its wide popularity from its basic passive, nonirritative flavor.

Next door is Japan: small, aggressive, hostile, creative, and energetic. Japan has always been the masculine thorn in the side of the massive and mostly nonresistant Orient. Reasons for these different roles probably arise out of agrarian and economic necessity, as well as deeply rooted and long-practiced culture patterns. Nevertheless, the role polarity is obvious, and each nation sits in modern history as a commentary on the type of gender it symbolically represents. Although China is overrun with revolutionary Communism, whose basic tenets are directed mainly toward aggressive nations, the chances appear very strong that the theory of Communism will never see fulfillment in Chinese culture. This is due principally to the sheer vastness of China, and also to the fact that that nation has a tendency to absorb, dilute, and ultimately devalue any aggressive intervention in its traditionally maternal mores. Japan, on the other hand, which has dared to intrude into the privacy of the other parts of the world, has displayed male aggressiveness, and now exists as a nation quickly adjustable to the instrumentalities of Western twentieth-century culture, yet with an Oriental independence about making up its mind, and maintaining a uniqueness and stubborn self-preservation among the nations. True, both nations survive, which indicates that either gender-role has within it the essential vitality of remaining alive. However, the world's largest nation is contributing comparatively little to the current trends of thought and relevant solutions to human problems, while in its flank a much smaller nation carries strategic influence far beyond its boundaries.

It takes no effort to transpose this similarity into the ecclesiastical scene. Christianity is statistically the largest religious community on earth, known in some measure within every country, and widely accepted as a fact of life both east and west. No longer the creator of culture, or the judge of men, or the inspirer of national policy, the Christian church (and this most especially in the Protestant genre) simply waits to enfold those who would seek sanctuary within its mumbled promises.

Gouging into the flank of the church is the smaller but more vocal, and somewhat bothersome but aggressive, community of Communism. Aflame with certain concerns over the human predicament, convinced of doctrinaire answers and technologically definable methods, similar to Christianity in that it is a community with a conviction, a purpose, and an eschatological hope, Communism relates to Christianity as the masculine irritant rather than the peer rival.

That both contain the elements of survival is rather evident. The necessary doctrine of coexistence requires that each find its unchallenged opening in the loyalties of the strong leadership of the world. Were both to occupy the same gender-role, such as masculine-masculine, coexistence would be impossible and a rivalry of worldwide proportions would always be in order. Coexistence can be possible only when these two forces calling for the loyalty of men can appeal to different dimensions in the same personality, namely, that one demand the loyalty of aggressive, creative, active protagonism, and that the other simply be a sanctuary to which man can repair to lick his wounds and find succor.

It is possible that the subtle psychology of historic tradition is already predetermined in the direction of the church's maintaining its feminine and therefore less relevant role. However, just as in the medical affirmation that femininity contains certain elements of masculinity, and vice versa, just so is it the thesis of this writer that there are enough elements of masculinity within the church that it may with integrity assume such a place of positive leadership and authoritative proclamation as indeed to enter into direct competition with the other voices of the twentieth century that claim the prime allegiance of man.

Yet, surprisingly, the church as it is, exists; even more, it grows and, apparently, thrives. Each new suburb soon boasts its new, young, growing cluster of attractive, contemporary, busy parish chapels. Though the blighted urban areas seem content to let their crumbling houses of worship deteriorate apace, the hyperactive middle class still insists on raising stucco temples to accompany the schools, parks, and sky-rise apartment houses. A superficial glance would tend to make one feel that the church is amazingly aggressive, penetrating modern life at the grass roots.

Before such a conclusion gets too assuring, it is rather important to list the strong unseen determinants that affect the life of the church areligiously. These forces, undercurrents of the sociological facts of life, tend to give impetus to the "success" of the church without necessarily contributing to its purposes, giving a deceptive impression of effectiveness. These factors, combined with a strangely subtle situation we shall call "factor Beta," may partially explain the church's deserving the feminine image without seeking it.

Looking at the representative residential parish church, alerted by the insights of Berger, Winter, Fry, and others, we see the following several influences at work:

The "organization plus" factor. Especially strong in suburbia, this is the tendency to express any kind of commonly held goal in easily visible structures with status-awarding positions of leadership. Probably because the type of mass production and planning that made possible the fantastic conveniences of the middle-class economy has become the most widely heralded *modus vivendi,* there is the community compulsion to organize, elect officers, and struggle for feelings of accomplishment and worth. Whether the effective motive is really to fulfill the conscious stated goals (such as P.T.A., service clubs, political party clubs) or to find publicly accepted activities in which to search for associations of non-judgmental support, it remains true that this is a strong contributory element to the success of any movement in the neighborhood milieu.

Studies of newly organized suburban Protestant churches in the mushrooming new fringe communities of megalopolis show that perhaps the easiest of all the preliminary duties in beginning a new parish is that of forming basic and subsidiary organizations, drawing up constitutions and bylaws, establishing constituencies and electing officers. It is also true that there is usually rather rapid turnover in the first few years of the immature developments in any new church; however, the organizational integrity provides a backbone within which the organization can survive though the membership changes. It is not always important that the stated objectives of the

Thus the church inherits from the modern mind an undeserved, and not necessarily helpful, public approval.

The "religious plus" factor. The severe orientation toward the technological, provoking the adulation of the faceless machine as the patron saint of all that we stand for, has not in any way accounted for the sense of the mysterious and metaphysical which is common, in varying degrees, to all men. The rather ready following that practically all movements seem to solicit, whether dealing with the religious or the occult, is evidence here. In a world in which nearly all our questions concerning the physical world are getting elaborately documented and valid answers, the modern man is uncomfortably aware of the other questions which he cannot totally succeed in repressing.

Here we approach one of the anomalous embarrassments of the church. Loyal as it is to institutional rationalism, the church cannot hide the fact that it is based upon certain supernatural assumptions or revelations. The more mysterious aspects of faith, prayer, belief, the difficulties of interpreting certain nonrational passages in the Bible, and the problem of even discussing the theological anthropology of Jesus, usually constitute the insolubles and divisive predicaments of parish life. Where the leadership of a local church is theologically sophisticated, capable of euphemistic interpretation, and courageously deals with human involvement in "things unseen," here is the church that has the most questions raised, and by far the most questions left unanswered. Official boards are usually embarrassed to clutter up their deliberations with any implications of Bible study, and elected church leaders are most often threatened by the implication that they should also be religious leaders and teachers. The fringe groups of Protestantism usually solve this problem by being unashamedly supernatural, and content to express this aspect in simplified formulas and prescribed devotional activities, asking fewer rational questions and participating more intensely in emotional expression and simplified, austere, moralistic behavior.

This may demonstrate the possibility that modern man is hungrier for courageous and socially supported exploration into the nature of God and His eternal intentions than the leadership of the church itself! However, inasmuch as the church is the only organization that formally points itself in this direction, it accumulates considerable popular interest.

One of the psychic problems to which no authoritative scientific voice is addressed is secular eschatology. Now that atomic power is accepted as being possibly world-destructive, the problems of human destiny course in some manner through every man's mind. The massive frustration that is the inevitable end of prosecuting this line very far is a tremendous force toward some symbolic approval of the church. Any idea, no matter how fantastic, is better than the individual's having to work it out for himself. This, incidentally, is a direct result of a culture that makes high priests of our scientists, sacred vestments of the laboratory white coat, and the Holy Monstrance in the test tube. We will listen to anyone who seems clinically authoritative rather than to our own questionable ideas.

The "post-Protestant plus" factor. The mostly mythological memory of a church-flavored society hangs over suburbia like a heavy fog. The nostalgia of the quiet Middle Western town, with the swinging church bell, the friendly folk, and the father-figure village parson who smiled benignly at our Scripture recitations, is detectable practically everywhere. Because the sanctity of this precious memory approaches the totem, a neighborhood without a church is unthinkable. And the more it resembles the dream, the better.

Even more inviolable is the Bible as a security symbol. Somehow it contains the answers, though it's perfectly impossible to read, and the family history tucked between the Testaments is the contemporary equivalent of burial beneath the church floor. Because it mediates the good life, it is to be exalted, especially by some organization that appears to understand it.

Recent Supreme Court decisions delineating separation of church and state, accompanied by official denominational statements of major Protestant churches, have brought most interesting cries of bewilderment and dismay from probably widely representative Protestant lay leadership across the country. This bewilderment is based upon the unconscious identification of Protestant culture with the nature of the church. Observations by many that these decisions are "secularizing" and "de-Christianizing" our country are based upon the assumption that faith is supported by society, which is affirmed and enforced by political and legal structures. If this is not true, this logic continues, the church is thrown to a decided disadvantage. Or, to put it more succinctly, a culture that does not produce and support the values of the church, thus deliberately rejects the church, and implicitly, because the church is the weaker of the two in ultimate strength, complete paganism can be the only result. Examination of this line of reasoning points up rather acutely that the very strong force of the post-Protestant sentiment not only brings considerable membership and money to the church but actually also works very strongly for its destruction as a noncultural, or masculine, force.

The "denominational program plus" factor. This may be where the lack of definition of a local parish suffers its greatest blow. This is where the Roman Catholic Church becomes more churchly—that is, both pastoral and prophetic, in undergirding the local sacramental life with regional, multiparish teamwork. But Protestant life, oriented not so much around the universal Sacrament as the charismatic (more or less) congregational leadership, bleaches out in widespread projection, developing a rather strong ecclesiastical colonialism. Worldwide Communion is a remarkable and laudable exception.

Notable examples of well-developed projections of collective righteousness, and bearing an obvious affinity to the healthy capitalistic respect for cause-and-effect mechanisms, are the Protestant promotional programs. Usually geared to promote big thinking in a "representative" parish, they of necessity bypass any coping with the real problems in the actual local reference, such as interpersonal relations. Yet, because of the administrative mechanical anonymities, were any local minister to remain no more than the faithful intermediary of the suggestions from above (and I don't mean heaven), he is a guaranteed success. Carefully avoiding any kind of personal reference, except to the pocketbook, never dealing with devotional necessities (well, *hardly* ever), emphasizing institutional loyalty, these provide a covert from the storm of associations of pastoral meaning.

These "plus" factors guarantee a readily visible success to a programmatic church in suburbia. But since they bear practically no relevance to the basic nature and purposes of the church, they eventually generate as much of a threat to its integrity as they do a help. This is the power struggle of which I speak: the typical church has a built-in impetus of extraordinary force, attributable in no way to the veracity of its creed, and liable at any time to subvert the gospel whenever it seems to interfere with resolving these other goals. Seen in this light, the local church becomes a sociological crossroads, a theological disaster area, a victim of its own unidentified hidden agenda.

Psalm CLI

"To be chanted after the solemn reading of the budget"

O sing unto the Lord an old Song,
One that He hears over and over again;
The song of the mighty, with power and wealth,
Who live in fatness and the abundance of possessions,
Whose tents have thick carpets and hosts of electronic
　　servants,
And who say,
"Behold, we cannot give more.
We must feed our overfed children,
And buy overpowered cars,
And maintain our fantastic standards,
Though we don't care to reason why."

O give praise unto a God who lets us get away with it;
Who answers our cries of empty self-pity
Not with thunderings
And lightnings
Of a God of wrath judging His own
Who think they can live in a world
Of suffering
And loneliness
And lostness
And hostility

And horrible, devastating war
And not care enough to love and to give.
O give thanks unto Him
Whose only rebuke
Is the silence
And our own conscience.

Great and Mighty is our God,
And greatly to be praised,
For He watches us
Decrease our giving
Withdraw our involvement
Lessen our pain
Crawl into our beautiful stone shell
Through the wide, tearful eyes
Of a hundred thousand hungry children,
Through the narrow, hostile faces
Of the craftsmen of international conspiracies,
Through the nodding sarcasm of disillusioned youth,
And He says nothing.

Praise ye the Lord!
Praise Him upon the high-sounding instruments.
For even as we lust after the enchantments
Of much goods,
And conformity,
And pledge our lives to the tin gods of possessions,
And pledge no excellence to our faith,
Even so does He permit us.

But though He be silent
Yet doth He follow after us.
An old scene is repeated.
There is the sound of nails into flesh into wood.
And a sigh in the dark.
And grace.

From the *Kirk Journal,* The First
Presbyterian Church of San Rafael, California

II

FACTOR BETA:
TOWARD A SPLIT-LEVEL
MEMBERSHIP

Four hundred years of Reformation history have brought many lessons. Some of them have confirmed the integrity of the Protestant movement and brought refreshing vitality to the Christian witness. But some of the dogmatic Reformed ideas, especially concerning the nature of the church and the ministry, have yet to accept the lessons of reality.

Experience is an exacting teacher. It not only establishes the suppositions that are right, by showing they can "wear well," but it can make a misguess rather chronically annoying. Since the non-Roman Christians have never dealt honestly with the doctrine of tradition, they must pay the price of working out their historical lessons by the painful insight of hindsight.

Thus, the point that must be made here is not new or earth-shaking, just too timidly identified and overwhelmed by a custom that doesn't want to see it. It's almost too obvious to belabor, yet becomes the main point in any consideration of the church's being a disciplined community.

We can call it "factor Beta." It is exactly the reason for the Roman Catholic bifurcation of clergy and laity. But beware lest our shibboleths about preserving the "ministry of the laity" divert us from the all-important real reason.

This factor is the simple, plain fact that within the recognized corpus of the church there are two quite different kinds of people—or at least two different sets of motive patterns. It would be inaccurate to separate them into "leaders" and "followers," yet that has a small amount of accuracy. Perhaps the most indicative statistic to begin with is the giving profile of a standard-brand suburban church, which tells its own significant story. Church X has three hundred pledging "units." A simple graph showing numbers of givers and sizes of donations, instead of having any ascendant symmetry to it, will look like a double-humped dromedary, with the hump on the left showing a large number of people whose gifts cannot, under any consideration, reveal any more than a mild token involvement with the purposes of the church. And, of course, the hump on the right will show a small number (usually from 10 to 15 percent of the total) whose giving may amount to 75 to 90 percent of the church's support.

Our classic strategic error for centuries has been to assume that this figure means no more than that there are people who need to be exposed to more carefully planned stewardship drives. Thus, undeserved pain appears in feelings of guilt, self-accusation, or scornful hostility around the circle of church officers. It is my contention that this is the most obvious indication of a situation in the Protestant local parish today, in which the other evidences will be far more ambiguous, which is our greatest unsolved problem. We go blissfully on, incapable, perhaps because of stubborn doctrinaire reasons, of admitting that we are ministering to (or with) *two separate levels* of parochial life. This I see as a lack of definition of the local parish in existential reality. Since, then, we are unwilling, or unable, to represent to ourselves or to the public at large, the distinguishing characteristics of the church, and because we are riding rather heavily the contemporarily popular bromides of the "lay ministry," we have deliberately ignored a fact of life that lets centuries of classical experience go unseen. We are also giving a homogenous, and therewith inadequate, type of pastoral care.

The early church knew this factor clearly, and the symbol of it became the rood screen, the reed narthexes that divided the catechumens from the baptized Christians. From the early second century, as we shall document later, there is ample historical evidence that the church understood its uniqueness in the world clearly enough to point out the difference between the pushers and the riders, acknowledging both but opening only part of its worship life to everyone, reserving its sacramental life to the confirmed membership. As the centuries went by, and the church developed rather large objectives in its world confrontation, it generated inevitable impatience with the passivity of the majority in the bleachers and evolved the highly justifiable and practical terms of "religious Christians" and "secular Christians." There were, on the one hand, those who wanted to effect the radical demands of the gospel on the world, and, on the other hand, those who were content to see the church as endowing the common life with a pious but undemanding assurance. It is apparent that if the church had not developed its own ecclesiastical aristocracy, it would have been paralyzed and ineffective. To translate this into the cleavage between clergy and laity today, that is, to think that this has produced a dangerous dichotomy of professional and amateur Christian, is to miss the real dynamics of seeing the church genuinely trying to be obedient and theologically honest at the same time.

The church has naturally developed its own language, its own intramural conversation. To the two different halves of this factor, the language comes through in remarkably different settings. Our own family semantic problem is nearly catastrophic because of the different frames of reference in which the language of the church is heard. Picture a community in which the words "street lights" mean "pocket flashlights" to a majority of the citizenry, and see how rational a bond election for street lighting would be. This is the situation in a local church surrounding such words as "prayer," "tithing," "witness," "Christian concern." And its cause is not so much the need for an ecclesiastical lexicon as a clarification of the community in which these words are the lingua franca.

Look at the parish today. Made up, usually, of a small inner core of believers who assume the necessary posts of leadership with gratitude and devotion (albeit frequently naïve), and surrounded by a cloud of uninvolved and mildly approving witnesses, it can move in no prophetic direction "as the church" without doing great interior battle with the forces of inertia, practically sealed in by the religiously immobile whose grasp of the meaning of the church is something less than courageous. No local parish is free to be a church, in the sense of a community holding unspoken, deeply valid affirmations to action, because of sheer tons of dead weight. This is not so much a problem of Christian education, or evangelism, but rather, a definition of the church.

The first realization of this hard truth of life appears in the Scriptural record of the early church. In the book of The Acts we see that the church had already been handicapped by attracting large numbers of people who were coming along for a free ride, and in this case, a free meal. The church did not close its doors on them, nor refuse to acknowledge that they may be genuine parts of the church as a whole, but it immediately, and with the accuracy of its own desperation to be true to its message, identified the problem. It was necessary to make clear the separateness of functions within the church, giving recognition to the apostles and the deacons as being the "cutting edge" of the church in the world, recognizing that the majority comprised a large resource from which other kinds and future leadership might eventually come.

This was simply saying that there are different kinds of Christians in the church, and with amazing administrative sensibility, making provision for the two kinds to be clearly and nonjudgmentally recognized!

Aided, as we have already seen, in the apostolic times by the sacramental delineation, and later in medieval times by the differentiations of Holy Orders and the institutionalized asceticism, the church has actually faced every age with a certain measure of adjusted insight as to the different levels of its constituency, and an effective measure of organization to give both recognition and relevance to the practices of the church in the world. This is the one greatest glaring inadequacy of the Protestant phenomenon of the twentieth century.

Having mistaken the basic thrust of the Protestant Reformation as being directed toward the alleviation of a non-Scriptural discrimination, we have compounded the felony by insisting that the church is and has always been, in its greatest and purest essence, a homogenized community. This inclusive homogenization always of necessity leads to either the hollow shell of an ineffective discipline or the more honest situation of no discipline at all. And when the church continues to practice existence as a single body with no understanding of its levels of devotion, it develops a deliberately ignored, tragic cleavage.

As a matter of fact, the cleavage only becomes the more dismal as successful educational standards get more sophisticated. Ministers are getting more erudite, the circle of lay leadership is tending to be more thoroughly trained, making the gulf, and therefore the tension, ever wider. In my city of San Rafael, I am watching the phenomenon of the local Roman Catholic Church working earnestly at the deepening of the lay apostolate and training significant numbers of non-clergy to take places of leadership in church and community. Since this is really an adaptation of Protestant theory, not arising out of the centuries of experience, and since it ignores factor Beta, which the Roman Church has formerly acknowledged, I fear the development of unforeseen problems. The clear role identification that has given the church effective power is now assuming some of the ambiguities of factor Beta. The one glimmer of hope is in the adamance of the hierarchy to cling to its basic affirmations about the uniqueness and high calling of the church itself. (Perhaps a translation of the classical vows to the lay apostolate would keep the situation from complete chaos.)

We are frequently called, either by conscience or by denominational programs and necessities, to promote certain causes within our congregations. These range all the way from special offerings or fund drives to social and political action. Is it not strange that most of these do not arise out of the essence of the local church, but have to be superimposed? Is it not a serious matter that this always involves a great deal of administrative arm-twisting that usually results in meaningful response from only a minority?

The fact is that we *do* have, and have subtly encouraged, two classes of Christian citizens. We have apologetically eliminated all sanctions of external discipline, thereby giving notice to the world that a halfhearted response to the gospel is better than none, and created the monstrosity of a church dominated by the mildly attracted. It is as though the planning committee for next year's Rose Bowl game found itself to be doctrinally embarrassed by the necessary delineation between players and spectators, and announced that anyone coming next New Year's Day was welcome to that enormous stadium, and could either play or watch, as he wished, with little discussion as to his qualifications to do either. Not wanting to be judgmental or disciplinary, yet knowing that the game ought to be played (it always has, you know), the committee finds that the only workable solution is to let the Mighty Spirit of Football dwell on the hearts of the crowd, and let the ones who think they can, who think they are ready and able, come down to the field, so that everyone can go home with the feeling that we were all equally welcome, and we all played the game. Admittedly, this is a ludicrous analogy, but it does raise a question about the validity of training, selection, and the use of authority and power to make the event worthwhile.

It only requires a look at two of the areas of church life, with the foregoing illustration in mind, to see the process of near self-cancellation involved in factor Beta. First, the functions of the church: those pointed inward, such as Christian education and leadership training. In all other fields of endeavor where important issues are at stake and national and international problems are under consideration, the whole complex of education is always entrusted only to trained professionals, who have the competence in their field that comes from the discipline of proper training and preparation. Not so in the Protestant Church; even though there is now a cultus of seminary-trained "directors," well over 99 percent of all the parish educational functions in the local church are maintained by willing volunteers, and in the majority of cases there has been little or no research into the qualifications or preparation of such instructors. In subjects of such life-touching relevance as Biblical exegesis, the church interprets itself at the local, and therefore most widespread, level, chiefly through the lives and voices of minimum preparation and discipline. How the church can survive such a surrender to unguided subjective opinion may perhaps remain one of the unexplained miracles of Christian history.

Second, the witness of the church: Before the gathered community, the bishop or presbyter or ordained minister rises to preach the gospel. To whom does he preach? If he brings his interpretation to any level of Biblical sophistication, so that he may feel that he can deal with relevance and depth to the issues, he has in one stroke deleted 90 percent of his congregation. If he reserves his preaching to be an actual act of communication to the majority of his listeners, therefore being also in some measure effective to the outside, nonchurch world, he is feeding his people a starvation diet of spiritual truth.

Factor Beta goes completely disregarded in the Protestant local parish; or even worse, its obviousness is troublously repressed. Yet the orthodox and more experienced parts of the church have met this with simple honesty. Let those who are stirred by the Holy Spirit have at it! Make provision for them to give their lives in study, or prayer, or Christian action, or evangelism, or teaching the gospel, as holy vocation. And for the majority of those who are content with the Christian flavor as a happy explanation of the imponderables, erect a system with obvious, simple, and pastoral opportunities for the alleviation of guilt, and a nonjudgmental acceptance. And let the line of difference be clearly drawn, so that we may play our separate roles without the uncertain complication of ambivalence. And say what you must, this has clarified and released rather remarkable power.

The Protestant tradition, being a direct reaction to the Roman Catholic abuses, suffers from its own extreme overstatements. We protested in great agony at the symbolism of the church with its nave for the secular Christians, and its choir-sanctuary for the disciplined clergy, and clamored for the rood screen to come down, that we may all sit in the chancel with equal access to the Holy Table. Realistically, it appears as though we have *dragged the whole Christian community out into the nave,* and cry with great pains of rejection when any of our company dare wander into the sanctuary, that the mythical ministry of the laity is being violated!

Factor Beta means that the local parish, and this seems to be most acutely true in the Protestant setting, only achieves any kind of unity or comity on the level of the *lowest common denominator,* and will always be limited to this as long as the factor goes unfaced. Someone has said that the Protestant Church is antiurban; I would say it is antireality. Dreams of improving this by programmatic innovations, such as theologically enlightened study groups, will only serve to increase the intracongregational tensions and *put the sharpness of the conflict within the church when by all rights it should be between the church and the world.*

The problem is one of definition. The church is called the fellowship of believers in Christ. But we fear with a monumental dread to deal critically with just what is meant by a "believer." And since the essence of local parish life is unconsciously dedicated to the proposition that the only safe judgment on this is subjective, we enforce and support a passive vagueness that rests entirely on the assumed and unspoken.

I see no compromise whatever with Protestant principles in dealing with factor Beta. As a matter of fact, the predicament of the parish church is the result of our cowardice to be honest to our own standards. Simply put, I suggest we move the believers (which will necessarily mean only those who are willing to go) out of the nave and into the chancel. Then, significantly, we must turn around and give some kind of theologically respectable recognition to those who stay in the nave. If the necessary support comes from the authoritative higher church courts, we *can* erect meaningful standards for membership. Admittedly, this will thin the ranks, probably by considerable numbers, but I seriously doubt if our institutional securities really do depend on a broad base of popularity. Since the real area of bewilderment here is what to do with those who are left behind without seeming cruelly exclusive, we need to consider reviving the old "learner" or catechumen classification of premembership (or nonmembership) and let it have the status of being a majority group. Then let the church be *the church!*

This, then, is the situation. The church of Jesus Christ exists in history, and is alive. In our framework, however, it is more a victim than the originator, more a derivative from powerful secularities than the framer of values. The church's voice is (and the world knows this better than we) usually a squeaking echo of what other voices have already said.

Yet I rise to say here that there is no alternative to the church's being relevant, and we can use the very determinants indicated here to the glory of God. Given a church leadership aware of the treachery of the plus factors, and willing to work with factor Beta as a fact of life, we could be ready to begin the next great Christian era. It may well be that Protestantism as such has run its course, and made its point, and can be retired in favor of a new classicism that would appear in the parish in certain specific, visible ways.

At eighteen years of age [Dwight L.] Moody desired to join the church and presented himself for membership. It was no easy matter to join a church in those days because a rigid examination was given to all applicants. The record of the board concerning Moody reads much like a modern social worker's case history: "No. 1,079. Dwight L. Moody. Boards, 43 Court Street. Has been baptized. First awakened on the 16th of May. Became anxious about himself. Saw himself a sinner, and sin now seems hateful and holiness desirable. Thinks he has repented; has purposed to give up sin; feels dependent upon Christ for forgiveness. Loves the Scriptures. Prays. Desires to be useful. Religiously educated. Been in the city a year. From Northfield, this State. Is not ashamed to be known as a Christian. Eighteen years old." . . . He was refused.

Leo K. Brown, *The Private Devotional Lives of Finney, Moody, and Spurgeon* (Privately published, San Rafael, California, 1963)

III

WHAT SHALL THE CHURCH REQUIRE OF THEE?

So, there we are! We've gone and said it, even put it into print! Let's say it again: there are two kinds of people within the church, religious Christians and secular Christians. And, in the saying, we have opened a veritable Pandora's box of many questions, to all of which there are no simple answers. Frankly, it would have been much easier to leave the lid closed.

How do we tell these two categories apart? Where is the authority to say? How does one even start without being seduced into oppressive legalism? Does not just the mention of it invite the possibility of Pharisaism dominating the life and thought of the church? Who shall receive the Sacraments —all, within the church, or simply those of the advanced group? What will be the nature of church life at the local congregational level if this distinction is given recognition?

It must be noted that judgment can never be avoided within the corporal integrity of the church, especially pertaining to the question of membership in the church. All churches have certain discriminatory practices prescribed by which it can be easily determined who is, and who is not, a member of a certain communion. Though some of these practices refer to the accident of birth, or to geographical jurisdiction, or to inherited traditions, at least an equal number of modern Protestants have token machinery of sorts by which the voluntary application for church membership can be processed, usually the pressing of the question relating to belief or faith in Jesus Christ as Lord. Some churches append the whole decision on sacramental fulfillment, i.e., all those who have received the Sacrament of Baptism are members of the church, thereby clinging to a simple and visibly mechanical symbol that tells its own story. Others, including the mainstream of American Protestantism, rotate the judgment around a confession of faith, either formally creedal or subjectively expressed. Very few Protestant churches acknowledge people as members who have not in some way voluntarily identified themselves with Christian theology, belief, life, or practice.

Therefore, all churches are already judgmental. This means that the question is not, Shall we become judgmental and erect external standards of delineation on the matter of being a Christian? but, Are our present discriminatory standards adequate? The Christian church cannot afford, in an "age on ages telling to be living is sublime," to be nonqualitative in its affirmation concerning the people involved in its witness. No present system of church government permits this. The question, then, is not whether or not the Sermon on the Mount is being violated by erecting some structure of judgment, but whether that judgment is relevant.

It is, then, appropriate to undertake here a study of what it has meant, across the centuries, to be a member of the Christian church. Definitions of the church are plentiful, usually rather doctrinaire, and in all cases rooted more in systematics than in existential reality; this is quite in order since any definition of the church is both a description of an extant fact and an eschatological hope of the church that is coming but not yet fully arrived. However, certain aspects of that church are very much rooted in time, and in these aspects subtle definitions are held. Thus, to define the church is to lap over into a regime outside of time, for the church exists there. But to define what it is to be a member of the church, in the order of this world, is to state what the finite and worldly side of the church is. So, in a way, it could be said that here we attempt to find out what the church really is, in history, by examining its standards of belonging.

We shall not concern ourselves too much with definitions of membership that arise out of sacramentalism, i.e., that a Christian is one who has received the ritualistic ministry of the church, for this standard has not so much asked the question, How has he qualified to become a Christian? but, What has happened to him? We want to know what has been required of him first. Nor will we deal much with the polemics on confirmation and Baptism, for these are procedures of entrance, not standards. Further, we shall not discuss the structure of internal discipline, such as penance and excommmunication, for these relate to those who are already in the church.

Rather, this inquiry presses the question, What kind of person becomes a member of the church of Jesus Christ, and what evident change in his manner of living is required by his becoming a part of the church?

We are well aware of the struggle of the apostolic church in the so-called Council of Jerusalem related in Acts, ch. 15, which was the infant church's first great critical episode. The subject there was the subject of this inquiry. The interpretation of that debate has thoroughly sidetracked the real issue. Shall uncircumcised, that is, people of a non-Jewish orientation, be permitted to become members of the new Jesus cult? Classically, historians have tended to read into this a procedural hassle, when it really deals with the much more profound and relevant question, Who is rightly prepared to deal with the demands of the gospel? Peter and the "circumcision party" were holding out for the new converts to experience first the living dynamics of Jewish monotheism, and were rightly concerned that those coming from other starting points might move in with none of the sense of reverence and majesty for God that was the hallmark of the Jew. This was a discussion, not on *how* converts shall be admitted, but on *what* is a rightly prepared convert.

The open-ended decision that culminated this council (let Paul go his way, and Peter his) was undoubtedly made in the light of the eschatological urgency that was the atmospheric intensity of the church of that day, rather than a letting down of standards, but in that the question was not directly answered, the church, as this study will show, has suffered to this day from an erosive ambivalence about membership standards.

This is not to say, of course, that there were no standards at all from apostolic times. It was the mark of the church that "much was demanded" from those who responded to the kērygma.

As long as a simple statement of belief or a willingness to be baptized in the name of Jesus Christ was all that was required for admission to the company there was but a single class of believers. But very early—as early as the beginning of the second century—a larger knowledge of the faith began to be required, and a certain course of training which was perhaps brief and simple at first, but, in the latter part of the second and the whole of the third century, became a widely organized and highly developed activity of the Church.[4]

This was the catechetical class or school; those who received instruction in it were catechumens. This is the training school for admission into the Christian church. It was in operation in Tertullian's day as it was in Pantaenus', Clement's, and Origen's.

It was, on the one hand, a bulwark of the church against unworthy members, on the other, a bridge from the world to the church, a Christian novitiate to lead beginners forward to maturity. The catechumens, or hearers, were regarded not as unbelievers, but as half-Christians, and were accordingly allowed to attend all the exercises of worship, except the celebration of the sacraments.[5]

Obviously, then, the early church felt that there should be a recognized and disciplined discrimination involved in permitting newcomers to attain full standing. Although the church was evangelistic, i.e., actively interested in winning the world to Christ, it realized that the order of the church was so startlingly different from the order of the world that care should be taken that those making the transition actually arrived safely, or did not arrive at all. Becoming a Christian was meant to affect, in visible ways, the life of the convert, and the church felt responsible to direct how this should be done.

The early church had a friendly, inclusive atmosphere. Kibitzers and inquirers were welcome, and curiosity was met with instruction. If such a visitor were converted, he approached the "teachers" of the church as a catechumen.

Then there came a serious testing; he had to declare what moved him to make the change and become a Christian, and his Christian friends had to give a sort of guarantee for him. Then his outer relationships in life were tested, and the first requirement laid upon him was that he should avoid every form of non-conjugal intercourse. If he were the slave of a Christian master, he must be recommended by that master as worthy of reception; if he served a pagan, faithful labor became a duty for him for the sake of the good reputation of the Christians.[6]

By this, we see that not only is *information* about the beliefs, teachings, and practices of Christianity a part of membership preparation, but also demonstrable evidence of change in ethical and moral directions is integral. Evidently the church felt that the quality of the lives of its constituents was a principal part of its witness to the world, and this was to be clearly understood at the entrance gate.

From the first there had been some moral cost attaching to membership in the Christian Society. In the case of the rich converts there was even some financial cost, not as of levy, but as of moral obligation, for the support of the custom of administering alms to the poor. . . . Then after he had been accepted as a candidate for instruction in the Christian tradition, he was expected to spend a large part of his time for the space of three years in preparation for his Christian duties.[7]

The priority, then, was first an evidence of a changed life, and second, instruction about Christianity. This last was no little item, according to the Apostolic Constitutions, which describe the curriculum as including knowledge of the Trinity, the order of the world's creation, series of divine providence: "Let him be taught why the world and man, the citizen of the world, were made; let him be instructed in his own nature, to understand for what end he himself was made; let him be informed how God punished the wicked with water and with fire . . . ; let him also be taught how the providence of God never forsook mankind, but called them at sundry times from error and vanity to the knowledge of truth. . . . After these, he must learn the doctrine of Christ's incarnation, his passion, his resurrection, and assumption, and what it is to renounce the devil and enter into covenant with Christ."[8]

It is interesting to note, as one scans this curriculum, how a major part of it is elemental Old Testament theology, the very content that the believer would have had if the Hebraic interests had won out at the Council of Jerusalem. At any rate, these entrance standards were so demanding, at least in their earlier interpretations, that there were two classes or kinds of catechumens: *audientes,* hearers—those who heard the Word of God, wished to become Christians, but were not yet looking forward to baptism; and *competentes*—those whose training was so nearly completed that they had given in their names for baptism and were being taught the great articles of the creed, the sacraments, and the penitential discipline of the church.

From the first it seemed right that only those who were of the inner circle should be present at the sacramental meal, what by the time of the Didache (ca. A.D. 90) was called the Eucharist, and others excluded. A place at the Holy Table was the claim only of the "proven" Christian, which meant not only a person who had exhibited satisfactorily his costly intentions, but who had also been able to keep himself "unspotted from the world," i.e., against whom no disciplinary action had been necessary. The separation of the gathered Christians, all of whom were welcome to the *synaxia,* or pre-Communion liturgy, was developed into a rather dramatic procedure.

The world had a right to hear the gospel; but those who have not yet "put on Christ" by baptism and thus as "sons" received His Spirit by confirmation *cannot* join in offering that prevail-

ing prayer. All who had not entered the order of the laity were therefore without exception turned out of the assembly after the sermon. The catechumens who had accepted the faith, but had not yet been added to the church by the sacraments, first received a special blessing from the bishop.
The deacons now proclaimed: "Let the catechumens depart. Let no catechumen remain. Let the catechumens go forth"; and when these had gone, cried again: "The doors! The doors!" as a signal to those of their number, or their assistants, who guarded the doors, to close and lock them against all intrusion. Then the church corporately fell to prayer.[9]

Thus far we have been describing the apostolic, patristic, and ante-Nicene church (before A.D. 325). This was the period of immense growth, both extensive and intensive. In this block of time, from the little company that had been present at Pentecost, it is estimated that the church had grown to number perhaps ten million. Classical persecutions, alienation within culture, the using of the church to make political and military advantage, all emphasized the otherworldly aspect of the church to its own advantage. So long as the church maintained that it was "not of this world" but belonged to a higher order, and required of itself a suitably high regimen, adversities only served to popularize it. And so long as standards of entrance were severely demanding, the outside world stood in respect, even though hostile. Not, of course, that the church was pure —far from it; the Christological controversies, the Gnostic and Pelagian heresies, were rending it asunder. Yet there was an integrity of content within the conversations, and those who stood around the Holy Table still paid a price to be there.

Then came A.D. 313, the year of the Edict of Toleration, which officially ended the Roman hostility against the church, and the backboard against which the church had been bouncing into shape dissolved. Constantine ascended the throne, making gentle overtures to the church in sentimental gratitude for military superiority. Roger Babson has rightly said, "The Church of Christ lost her purity the night she slept with Constantine."

Dom Gregory Dix more wistfully describes the beginning of deterioration because of the new sovereign:

The new emperor of his own accord publicly acknowledged himself in some sort a believer in Christianity, and proceeded as such to take his own political and administrative measures, without any organized consultations with the church. Short of refusing to accept him even as a catechumen on the sole ground that he was an emperor, there was nothing that the church could do in the matter but acquiesce.[10]

It is most interesting, for the purposes of this study, to note that it is at the very point of a downgrading of requirements for entrance, albeit it involved the emperor himself, that the greatest decline in all church history began. Commenting on the tenor of the church's attitudes at this crucial moment, Dix spells out the nature of its inclusive intentions:

The church always insisted that Christianity was intended by God for every man. Her measure of a Christian was simply "communion," *partaking* in the corporate act of *worship,* with the belief which qualified a man for this and the conduct which befitted it in daily life. The attitude of the world, not of the church, brought it about that exceptional gifts of character were required to be a good communicant under pre-Nicene conditions. The hunger of the world then was for martyrs, and from her communicants the church furnished them sufficiently for the world's need.[11]

As any novice in church history knows, with the advent of Constantine, the Council of Nicaea (A.D. 325), and the blessing of the Roman Empire upon the brow of the church, mankind's most fantastic wedding of church and the public domain was consummated, and Christianity was no longer resisted, no longer held to give a substantive accounting for itself, no longer backed against the wall, no longer required to be made up of people who were willing to nonconform. The subtlety of this corrosion was not immediately evident, however, for the long slide downhill in the effective integrity of the church continued with occasional reverses into the late medieval period.

At least, this is a time when the church had great difficulty defining itself as being any different from any other order of society. The notion that the limits of the church were coterminus with the empire, or national interests, slowly crept like a plague over the face of Europe. It was a time for settling theological controversy while neglecting qualitative responsibility. And this is reflected no more clearly than in the standards of entrance into the fold. Baptism was widely and indiscriminately administered by the bishops who were acting as servants of the state; confirmation, which has never been equated with adult ability or awareness, was given to infants, usually within a year or two after baptism; it was the Council of Trent in the sixteenth century that regularized the minimum age for confirmation at seven years. Because the church by public statute had to render pastoral care to all citizens, it was next to impossible to be exclusive on qualitative grounds.

The difference here is part of the whole problem of qualifications for church fellowship. . . . The motive of protecting the fellowship from pollution was in tension with the motive of restoring the sinful brother. Gradually the more liberal interpretation prevailed, and as the penitential discipline was systematized it ultimately made provisions for the reception of those guilty of the gravest offenses.[12]

A cursory glance at nearly eighty volumes on church history, including the classic ones, failed to turn up any indication that the medieval church dealt at all with the subject of membership standards. The customs of the pre-Nicene catechetical schools were continued mostly as traditions, but without the original meaning of training for sacrifice.

The deacons continued to proclaim the dismissal of the catechumens before the intercessory prayers as in the pre-Nicene church, but there were ceasing to be any catechumens to depart. By the seventh century, this, too, had become a mere form.[13]

Dix sees this deterioration as having a causal relationship to the corruption of the liturgy itself; he indicates that it is here that the word "communicant" first came to be used, instead of the proper word "the offerers." This goes along with a change in the status of the laity from participants in a corporate act with the celebrant to passive beneficiaries of and assistants at his act. These changes were not completed before the medieval period, and indeed constituted between them the essence of that medieval way of regarding the Eucharist which has proven so unfortunate in different ways all over Christendom. The evidence indicates that this lay participation, as part of the ministry of the Eucharist, dropped off because of fear of polluting the Holy Sacrament, so the people withdrew.[14]

Here, then, is a twist of history. In its struggle to retain some of the purity of its calling, the church in its earlier years felt that those who entered the gates of the church should be rightly prepared and forewarned, and that no one should be accepted without a clear realization of its "once for all" demands. This whole system was predicated on the church's ever remaining the otherworldly, unaccepted minority. When the catastrophe of political recognition occurred, and the emperor himself stormed the gates of the church, entrance standards became awkward and vestigial. The church fathers tried valiantly to restore integrity by compensatingly tightening the procedures of internal discipline, but the sheer weight of numbers within who had no image of commitment made most disciplinary actions eventually bizarre, irrelevant, and cruelly unjust. The last holdout for retaining the "inner circle" of those to whom Christ was Sovereign, the liturgy of the Eucharist, also gradually became diluted and like salt mixed with road gravel lost its flavor.

And it remains a fact, explain it how we may, that the passive receptiveness—the being reduced to mere listening—which was always necessarily the layman's role in the first part of the synaxis became his role also at the eucharist proper (which it had never been before) just in the period in which synaxis (open to the public) and eucharist began to be regarded as parts of a single rite.[15]

As the medieval phenomenon of Christendom developed, and the hostile tribes of Europe one by one bowed to the energetic missioners and accepted the cross, the method of entry was in politico-military units. When a heathen king was conquered, as his suzerainty fell, so also fell the tribal gods, and the clan or province was Christian. Individuals, especially the peasantry, were never consulted or challenged, baptism was administered wholesale by top-level negotiations, and the church instituted as one of the arms of government. The Holy Roman Empire, from Charlemagne to Charles V, needed no conversation with the people for religious consent; the church was its arm of culture-molding, and the sacraments, especially penance, the tools of control. So there could be no less relevant a subject for discussion during the long premedieval and pre-Reformation period than preparing for membership in the church.

It cannot be said that the concern for purity of witness was entirely lacking; undoubtedly the development of the second thrust of the ascetic movement, namely, monastic communities and Holy Orders, was part of the response of concern. And in effect, what these communities produced in their more advanced stages were churches in microcosm with adequate entrance standards. "Against this laxity," says Kenneth Latourette, "monasticism was a reaction and a protest."[16]

In his cursory summary "By Way of Inclusive Retrospect," Dr. Latourette is moved to comment:

As hundreds of thousands flocked into the Church and, in spite of the efforts of many zealous clergy, the lives of most Christians were not much if any better than those of the adherents of the surviving remnants of paganism, monasticism arose. Negatively it was a protest against the laxity of the main body of Christians and positively it claimed to offer a way of becoming perfectly conformed to the teachings of Jesus. Although at first the monks on the one hand and many of the bishops and clergy on the other tended to look askance at each other, monasticism soon became an integral part of the life of the Church.[17]

The monasteries could level their own requirements and discipline, and with the evolution of the classic vows of poverty, chastity, and obedience, proclaim their seriousness in a discipleship of quality. In reality, they became islands of little churches in a sea of ecclesiastical churchcraft. The use of the terms "religious" and "secular," even in the way our twentieth-century semantics has abused these words, more appropriately describes the context of the monastic phenomenon than we tend to think.

Since the church was in no position to exert the discipline of entrance requirements, all other attempts at general control and qualitative church life were doomed to failure. Suppose, for illustration, the medical profession were to lower its entrance requirements, so that anyone who was interested in the healing arts could be certified as a doctor and go into public practice. Then, in dismay over the subsequent malperformance of the profession, if the medical association were to control the situation by erecting standards of internal discipline, that is, committees to investigate each accused offender and punish him for not doing what he was never trained to do, the whole cause of the integrity of medicine would be utter chaos. Thus with the church: some saw simple membership as being a call to a healing ministry; most accepted it as a surface formality. Yet the world awaited significant and prophetic guidance from the church which, because of including people to whom the call to ministry had never been articulated, was *hors de combat*. Inclusive effectiveness was impossible; selective and functional relevance was the only alternative, and it was made possible through the different orders of monks. Indeed, they may well have saved the day!

The situation, historically, continues unresolved up through the early classical stages of the Reformation. True, Menno Simons and even John Hus had some creative suggestions to offer, but even Martin Luther was incapable of defining the covenant community of the church in terms separate from the politically provincial. Since the three original strains of the sixteenth-century Reformation all solicited their strength from governmental units, and pressed for reform, mostly in the area of the church's relation to Holy Scripture rather than its relation to world witness, the matter of qualifications for membership (or holy ministry) was an unimportant issue. It is true that this was the age of the great catechisms, but catechetical practices were more for nurture and apologetic, as well as

public polemic (see the Heidelberg Catechism, the Augs-
burg Confession) than for a process of induction and training.
In point of fact, of all the Reformers, Luther alone is concerned for education of the masses; his central theme of care
and nurture involved emphasis for the importance of education, the responsibility of parents in this enterprise, and the
responsibility of government to furnish free education. Of
course, these feelings were in historical context, in which
church-state liaison was a given, and the humanitarian motives
superseded ecclesiastical quality. So, in Luther's system, the
government must teach both secular and religious subjects,
because parents do not desire to do this, nor do they have
sufficient piety, nor are they qualified. It is up to the state to
compel education.

Calvin, it is true, was interested deeply in education, and
produced the Academy of Geneva. But his interest was always
directed toward the elite; higher education was for the aristocracy and the leadership, and the common people acknowledged their place by keeping out of the way. Although Calvin
worked more than any other Reformer for church discipline, he
hardly ever thought of its being involved at the door. Indeed,
he couldn't, for the public statutes of Geneva ordained the
obverse; anyone who wished not to be a part of the church
had to show cause before the town council, and be prepared
to take the consequences.

The first real examination of criteria for church membership since the ante-Nicene age is to be found in the so-called
"radical reformation." An example is the Marburg Anabaptist
Disputation of 1538, in which a debate was held with Bucer
and Eisermann representing the classical reformation, and
George Schnabel, Leonard Fälber of Maastricht, Herman
Bastian, and Peter Lose presenting the Anabaptist stand.[18]
Discussing the standard points at issue: baptism, the call of
the pastor, and magistrates, Schnabel stated that he had come
to the conclusion that "righteousness could be best secured
within small, self-recruiting, self-disciplining churches made
up of explicit believers independent of prince and magistrate
qua magistrate. . . . At the present time, he said, the most

conscientious evangelicals were being politically banished as separatists, while the state church in making only perfunctory use of the disciplinary ban was in effect compounding the dissatisfaction of the scrupulous and thereby augmenting the number of dissenters."[19]

The principal stand of the Anabaptists, as well as the other dissenters, was that a church should be the association of those who believe, and that none should even be baptized until he gave evidence of responsible faith in Christ. That this protest could not be completely ignored is seen in the ruling of the synod at Ziegenheim in November of 1538, which granted that " 'all baptized children as soon as they are old enough should be sent for [instruction in] the catechism, which shall be arranged in every place at such a time convenient for everyone sending the children.' "[20] A small condescension it was, but it did lead to constructive interchange between the Anabaptists and the state-church divines in Hesse.

The zeal of this new innovation in ecclesiastical thinking was greater than its content. It is well and good to require that new Christians be committed, but just how is this determined? The habit of the centuries, continued by the Reformation, was the memorization and repetition of a catechism, or by the affirmation of an official confession. The emancipated church of the radical right quickly recognized these as mechanical functions, which anyone with kinetic ability and a stale mind could fulfill. The emphasis then leaned toward subjective experience, witnessed to in primarily emotional terms, as seen especially in the words of John Wesley:

One circumstance more is quite peculiar to the people called Methodists—that is, the terms upon which any person may be admitted into their society. They do not impose, in order to their admissions, any opinions whatever. . . . They think and let think. One condition, and one only, is required—a real desire to save the soul. Where this is, it is enough; they desire no more. They lay stress upon nothing else; they ask only, Is thy heart herein as my heart? If it be, give me thy hand.[21]

The irony of this quotation is its hoped-for context, that is, that the Society called Methodists would be a subgroup in, and contributory to, the Church of England. Thus, a "given" which Wesley assumed, namely, that all those involved in his movement were already within the church, and that there would be a similarity to the separated communities within the church of the Middle Ages, never came off. So this, his original statement, is still used as the charter of The Methodist Church, an ecclesiastical entity of its own, as the standard for membership. The very goal toward which he worked, a revitalized church, was intended to be one with regimen and disciplined vitality. A great portion of Wesley's dream did come true, however, in an elite corps of people who were willing to live under discipline for the sake of the Lord, and give their witness to an experience of the Spirit. The stellar record of the Wesleyan revival at the beginning of England's industrial revolution, and the widespread influence of the circuit rider in America, bear rather impressive witness to the effectiveness of a movement oriented around a sense of ministry. The continuing witness of the Salvation Army, whose use of factor Beta is the most clearly honest in Protestantism, is a clear tribute to Wesley.

The story of church life in colonial America is so deeply rooted in classical Protestantism (Presbyterians in Pennsylvania, New Jersey, New York; high Puritanism in New England; Anglicanism in Virginia) that membership standards, still reflecting the Anglo-European confirmation-within-culture, went undefined, and actual church membership was comparatively meager. True, each church had procedures erected by which applicants were examined, but beyond the legal catechetical playbacks, or affirmation of a major creed, further questions became ridiculously moralistic and culturally primitive. The church's self-image during this period was that of the Great Restrainer; the New Age that Christ proclaimed was under way with bitter criticism in its teeth.

The struggle for purity of the eighteenth century was the Great Revival. Its first manifestations were entirely local, i.e., a church in a village set out to win the nonchurch members through covenants of prayer, witness, and special preaching services. Out of this grew the united meetings, then meetings between towns, and soon the mass appeal and traveling evangelists. The burden of this movement still carries forth the semantic of classical churchism; the word "revival" assumes that a prior claim, such as national edict, has been made upon the people for Christ, and now their volition was being appealed to so that they could "come back" to Christ! From the beginning many unexplainable bizarre emotional symptoms were observed, to the end that one testified to being "saved" by the marks of behavioral irregularity that the Spirit brought upon him.

This left the church suspended between the two horns of a dilemma. If it accepted the revivalistic witness as having made a valid claim upon the convert, then further examination of him would seem to question the efficacy of the Spirit, and all the patient processes of nurture would have been short-circuited. To insist that the Great Revival had to be subservient to the regular disciplinary process of the church, and maintain high standards of nurture and training, was to be "out of step." No less a personage than Jonathan Edwards was severely criticized, and finally forced to move from Northampton in 1749, because he dared to require more than a witness of the Spirit from some revival-converted applicants to the church of which he was pastor.[22] Horace Bushnell, a century later, was an articulate spokesman for sensible assessment of "Christian Nurture" within the family and the propagation of Christianity through family training and (by inference) selective breeding, as a direct antithesis to revivalism.

Of course, the great discovery of this conflict was the emergence of voluntaryism, in which church membership is delineated completely by the volitional choice of the people, with no sanctions of government involved whatever. The acknowledgment that church and state are separate orders of the common life, and are most free to be fully themselves when religion is not legally regulated, opened a whole new era of possibilities in ecclesiastical discipline that has yet to develop rightly.

In retrospect: in apostolic times, it was pragmatically necessary to be careful in admitting converts into the church, to be sure that they were prepared intellectually, emotionally, and subjectively to deal with the stringent situation of being a Christian. With Constantine, and establishment, the direction changed rapidly to a decision by government, and carried through into the Reformation, with monastic communities alone interested in selective discipline. The radical reformed groups once again introduced subjective volition, and qualification for membership depended on the applicant's meeting churchly approval. Disestablishment and voluntaryism have put the church back into the controlling position of requirement, but custom and history render the present practices rather weak.

The more conservative approach emphasizes that a church with charismatic spirit is its own standard.

Church growth depends on winning converts. Churches grow from nothing but converts—people who believe on Jesus Christ intensely enough to break with their past sins and cleave to Him as Lord and Saviour. Converts are not picked up lying loose on the beach. They are won by men and women whose own beliefs blaze hot enough to kindle faith in others. This involves the conviction that it is truly better for a man to leave father and mother and sister and brother, if need be, to obtain Christ. Church growth occurs more readily where churchmen believe that it makes an eternal difference whether one is a Christian or not and whether one's community is Christian or not.[23]

The churchly groups (to use Troeltsch's term) migrate more toward preparation classes, content teaching, the use of confirmation as reception ritual, and creedal criteria. But lack of strength and agreement among the churches, and lack of emphasis upon entrance as a place of high discipline, still leave the church open to dilution and ambivalent standards.

In a Presbyterian church, members are received into the church and dismissed from the church by the session and are subject to its discipline so long as they are members. . . .

Unbaptized persons are received into the church by vote of the session upon their profession of faith in Christ and their promise of obedience to him. This is followed by baptism. . . . It is clear that the reception into membership of The United Presbyterian Church in the United States of America is reception into the Church of Christ as a whole. For this reason it is not proper for a session to require more than the steps enumerated above from any person sincerely desiring membership, although the session may require attendance at such classes as it sets up and the undergoing of an examination as to Christian knowledge satisfactory to itself before accepting a profession of faith and also a promise of obedience.

Eugene Carson Blake, ed., *Presbyterian Law for the Local Church* (The Westminster Press, 1959), pp. 53–55

IV

PAGING SOLOMON!

Who shall make the decision? Wary of lopsided authority within the church, and tired of humans presuming to know the divine will, Protestantism has built within it a reluctance to say that any worldly system should point out the ground rules of Christian discipleship. But this is not to say that we have avoided the subject, nor that we are unprepared politically to deal with it. The constitution of the Presbyterian and Reformed churches, for instance, contains the clear mandate that there are ascending courts of authority, and that this very question, namely, membership, belongs squarely in the laps of these judicatories. Most immediate and responsible of them is the session, or board of elders, or consistory, in which the presbyters of the local congregation are clearly charged to examine every applicant for membership on the basis of his preparation to serve and follow Jesus Christ. To put into effect a realistic grappling with factor Beta, the Presbyterian Church for one does not need to change a single word of its already established law. In churches of episcopal power, the presiding officer may or may not have to consult with the ecclesiastical parliament under him, but in most cases is quite capable of clarifying and defining all who would be Christians in his diocese. In the Episcopal Church, where the bishop assumes personal responsibility for confirming every member in the entire diocese, he may, and is constitutionally enabled to, prescribe standards upon which he will consent to confirmation. So very little needs to be added to this type of church to determine the seat of decision, and originate a sensible definition.

In churches of congregational government, this will tend to be considerably more difficult, for no authoritative voice comes from outside the local parish. Individual heroic congregations, stimulated by the leadership of their more connectional brethren, may erect such standards of local parish worth as to inspire other churches of similar government to respond in kind. Here, as in so many historical developments down through the ages, it will depend on the churches of more centralized and efficient authority to set the pace, to color the prevailing characteristics of Protestant Christianity to the end that other individual congregations will be enlightened and inspired to follow.

But to return to a sample, such as a local Presbyterian parish, one can immediately see that its Calvinistic forebears were at least subconsciously quite aware of factor Beta, and sought to erect an ecclesiastical government that would permit a church of worthy discipline. Each local session must prescribe the meaning of membership in that particular church. Even though it is based on faith in the Lord Jesus Christ, and in assent to the demands of discipleship (without requiring verbal conformation to the formal confession of faith), each session assumes fully the responsibility for dealing with all the implications of Christian membership and making rather clear to all applicants what these implications would demonstrate in the life of that parish. In all cases where session authority to be selective has been challenged, the higher courts have supported the disciplinary and qualitative responsibility of the session.

There is, then, in Protestantism today already anticipated, the lines of responsibility in making the church qualitative. This needs no further questioning; rather, it needs proper and diligent use.

1. The criteria of difference to be used in judging between the secular and religious Christian needs very careful attention. Here is the area of biggest responsibility, and it contains

potentialities to a stifling legalism that could drive the church back to precisely where it is now, nonqualitative cowardice. Yet the present position is as fully untenable as is Pharisaism, and the possibilities for benevolent results in the life of the church invite us to at least give it our honest attention. Of course, one here will have to deal with definable externals, and find ways of giving rather clear evidence. I suggest there are four, at least, with great possibility for others to be developed as experience unfolds.

a. Preparation for Discipleship. This should include the following, all of which are minimum standards: a study course of five years between Baptism and confirmation, which would include at least two hours a week of study under professional tutelage, in each of two subjects: the first, a Biblical study, and the second having to do with the Christian witness, including both evangelism and social expression. This course of study needs to be augmented by examinations every six months by the session, or local ruling body designated to maintain this responsibility, with sympathetic understanding and a great deal of personal involvement among officers and learners. As the time of preparation draws to its close, the learner will be in advanced class, working closely with the clergy and members of the session, in considerable seminar-type dialogues on the relation of church to world.

b. Function. Here an apprentice relationship must be devised, in which each person preparing for church membership would be under the personal direction of some leader of the church, and involved in learning more about that function, e.g., teacher, youth worker, deacon, social worker, administrator, etc. Participation in a cell group, as described in Chapter X, is also a part of this apprenticeship.

c. The Rite of Ordination. Upon completion of these visible standards, and upon recommendation of those who know him closely, the person is to be examined thoroughly by the session in preparation for the rite of ordination. *The distinction between confirmation to membership in the church and ordination to the holy ministry must be erased,* and the two acts be welded into one and the same meaning. It shall have been given to be understood that the whole preparation has been for the response to the holy calling to ministry, and that this is the calling of Jesus Christ to all his disciples. Therefore, confirmation, or the laying on of hands to signify engrafting into the physical corpus of the church, shall be that act of visible witness to the answering of the call to service within the life of the believer. This need not vary in any way from the act of ordination to the professional ministry, with the exception that the latter be administered by a presbytery instead of by a session.

d. Recognition and Pastoral Care of Those Not Ordained. This is to be considered an area of great responsibility and opportunity, and if overlooked, can arouse such anxiety within the life of the church as to call for immediate relaxation of all disciplinary structures. The picture thus far shows two concentric circles, the small inner one comprising the disciplined and confirmed (ordained) leadership which is, rightly, the church. The much larger outer circle, containing the vast host of the "secular" or mildly interested, comprises the seedbed of the church. It is from this arena that the church is recruited; this is the context of conversion (see Ch. V). It is the primary call of the church to give pastoral leadership and nurture here, in order that the Holy Spirit may use whom he pleases; every ordained Christian is in some way involved in the ministry of service and care to the constituency. Token courses leading to "associate membership," or catechumen standing, which has neither the rite of ordination nor the right of voting on the principles and message of the church, must be given, with right praise and recognition for accomplishments therein. Requirement for admittance to the outer circle, the first experience of fellowship within the church, should be changed from a confession of faith in Jesus Christ, a much too mature experience to possibly be sincere or effective here, to an expression of interest in and loyalty to the historical church as it can be seen. A "halfway covenant" (as the Puritans called it), which involves the interested at their particular level of motivation without any inference of guilt for inability to believe, would be far more honest than the now embarrassing questions on theology and discipleship.

There are two dynamics of this possibility that must be emphasized. The first is that of ministry from the inner circle to the outer; the fear of being authoritative, judgmental, or exclusive can make the most earnest Christian wary of the "inner-outer" picture. Let it be affirmed that the church is servant, and that ordination is to service, not rank. The whole rationale of discipline and high preparatory and admittance standards is for *ministry,* and especially to those who yearn for Christ but are not yet involved. Thus, becoming a religious Christian is to accept the regimen of being a servant. The second dynamic is that of *motion;* to the picture of the concentric circles add fluidity, with constant intake into the larger outer circle from the uninterested world, and constant interrelationships within the unordained of evangelistic contacts, and hopefully, the eventual penetration into the inner circle of some. As one church officer, with whom this presentation was shared, commented from his own experience: "I stepped over that first low threshold, timid and resolved to keep my distance. I moved in the orbit farthest out, in only mild interest, until I was invited into a small study group, and was motivated to move inward. Now I will accept any requirement the church asks to prepare for service."

2. Since the Sacraments are, indeed, the instruments of the Holy Spirit, and since God's grace is conveyed through them in a manner no worldly church can direct, the Sacraments ought not to be restrained from the people under any set of restricting legalistic standards. Baptism is to be administered freely to those infants born into homes that are in some way connected with the church, either religious or secular Christian parents. The Sacrament of Holy Communion is to be offered always in open circumstances, with the invitation to all who confess Jesus Christ as Lord and Master to participate without prejudice. In effect, we are saying that the holy table should be moved not only to the front of the chancel but

actually down onto the floor of the nave, so that here, indeed, all those whose lives have been flavored by the sacrifice of Jesus Christ may come together in a unity that no worldly organization can divide. The point of difference between the two kinds of Christians in the church is not to be stressed here, rather the ecumenicity, universality, and eternal witness of the church are always to be shown forth. To adults who are interested enough in the validity of the church to seek some connection, Baptism is an appropriate beginning symbol, for it is the threshold of entrance into the household of God. Even as the Philippian jailer and his household were baptized in the middle of the night, on the basis of having had a valid experience of the power of the church, so too can Baptism be conscientiously administered to those who apply, though not yet qualified for holy ministry. Although it is true that under these circumstances many will be receiving the Sacraments though quite spiritually unprepared and intellectually inhibited, the central doctrine of the mediatorship of grace that each Sacrament represents must prevail. Indeed, that would not be far different from the present practice.

3. One would come to notice that the public life of the local parish church would be a very inclusive one, in which all people—religious Christians, secular Christians, and inquiring non-Christians—could feel warmly welcome. The services of public worship would continue to be largely on levels that communicate with matters that all neophytes could somewhat easily understand. There would always be the liturgical rehearsing of the gospel, as described in Chapter VI. As has already been noted, the Sacraments would be very available to the world. However, there would be further characteristics beyond those seen in today's church life. First, there would be a larger core of servants within the church who are actively engaged in furthering the mission of the church. Second, the obvious purpose of the church would be to effect the witness and message of the Lord Jesus Christ in all avenues of the common life of the community, rather than to be simply an institutional holding operation. There would be

active teams at work, surveying the community, addressing themselves to particular social problems and specific injustices, and bringing the Christian prophetic witness to bear upon them. There would be continuous traffic between the local church and many points of the mission field, both domestic and foreign, because the call to holy ministry would involve considerable activity in all the world.

Again, there would be a sense of *movement* from the casual inquirer to the accepting spectator, through confession of interest and Baptism, and further, then, into the disciplined preparation for holy ministry, to which all parts of the congregation would continue to feel an urgent and meaningful invitation. All the different functions in the life of the church would be under the leadership of those who had prepared themselves adequately for, and pledged themselves high loyalty and motivation to, the service of Christ as their chief vocation in life.

No great modification need be done as to the present arrangement of professional, i.e., full-time, theologically educated ministers, and other special preparation in other functions, though the great majority of those engaged in holy ministry will serve in remunerative posts outside the church, for the concept of difference would rest merely on function and expedience, and not upon any kind of ecclesiastical superiority.

4. The premedieval practice of holy orders and functional units within the life of the church, and ministering to it, will in all probability be *revived*. In point of fact, this revival is already under way. In the Protestant sphere, gospel ministers are lumped together in a special brotherhood of preachers and friendly commiserators, and represent the strongest single holy order now. In addition, there are in embryonic development, brotherhoods of Christian educators, church administrators, stewardship counselors, theologians, professors, chaplains, elders, and many other such. Were the already rather well proven evolutionary processes to be hurried up, one would see the eventual development of all these into special

functional segments, fraternities of committed Christians, some professional, and others not. Ordination to holy ministry can be accompanied by reception into a special order of functionaries, with its own additional disciplines and helps. The central development of each order and organization, along with the evolving of exclusive standards, will serve to augment and dramatize the choice to follow a holy vocation.

The present massive attempts at church school programs, involving overexpenditures for underused facilities, are gross waste. Let education be in two different categories, with appropriately different aims. Let a measure of basic discipline, at least up to the minimum of education anywhere else, be adopted; required attendance, more hours per week, professional teaching staff, and periodic evaluations (tests, grades, etc.). For the larger, or "catechetical" group, the whole curriculum is intended simply to set the stage within which a meaningful commitment is possible, and the ground rules of that commitment made rather clear, with the deliberate intention that those who cannot make such a radical step may continue in rosy incubation as long as they may need. For the core group, the confirmed and committed, a very different setting, unashamedly asking for prime time, effort, and loyalty, with a graduated scale of disciplines, devotional, civic, Scriptural, and didactic. Teaching of both groups is to be done *only* by the confirmed and qualified, even if there be only one such in a congregation; all other teaching is to be discontinued posthaste. Teaching of the second group is to be done only by professionals, or such volunteers as have had the equivalent of one year in seminary, and can be very innovative, using all the expressive insights of group relations, arts, research, and especially such relevant contacts with social issues as naturally develop out of the training. Only the second group would represent the church, and then always collectively.

Finally, it appears that the real age of the Christian church is just dawning. As the image of a disciplined community of covenant and calling becomes clearer, and all the proper methods of gaining integrity are enhanced, the church will become adequate.

The first and most fundamental revival needed in the Reformed Church is a revival of theological awareness and interest. Such an awareness and interest may be expressed by illiterate peasants wending their way back from sermon. Academic learning has very little to do with the recognition of the Church as our teacher. Once the teaching function of the Church is recognized, it is much easier for people to appreciate that the kind of education we receive from the Church is more than intellectual or artistic; it is education in Christian character, for the upbuilding of which a practical discipline is required that should make the training of a ballet dancer, for all its rigor, superficial by comparison. What is of primary importance to the Reformed Church in its present state is not that all should engage in such training; it is, rather, that the value and necessity of such training should be recognized as a condition of any advancement in sanctification. Not all are strong enough to bear the most rigorous kind of training in Christ; but so long as training in Christ is recognized by all as essential, the Church will accomplish its task. There is no place in the Christian Church for those who do not even conceive of their churchmanship in terms of any sort of training at all.[24]

It is rightly said, "When the gate is opened to the worthy, the household is safe."

Primarily, the first decision toward a qualitative and disciplined church must come from the superior courts. The General Conference, the General Assembly, or the Central Convocation, must through its authoritative structures state that the particular segment of the church over which that body rules is hereafter to be taking discipleship seriously, with discipline and direction. The next big stage after that will be the development in each local parish of a qualified ministry to train the subsequent ministries. It may be too glib to assume that in each local presiding professional minister or priest there is an adequate person to take such leadership. However, since he is in most cases the only man available, and in most cases unusually trained, here is where the local development begins. Armed with the authority of his denominational affirmation, a local minister can proceed in training and study, narrowing the brunt of his teaching ministry down to that small nucleus of those who will be courageous enough to begin.

Were I to repeat, for instance, an early experience of being the organizing minister of an entirely new parish in a new suburb, I would the second time proceed quite differently. To meet the stipulated requirements of having a local board of elders, we picked the six most worthy, however untrained, people in the congregation to be the first such officers. Now, that board would not come into existence until one or more persons in the congregation had completed a full and un-relenting course of preparation for entrance into the holy ministry. The completion of organization of such a congregation would await a qualified ministry there above and beyond the assigned professional. Whereas, thereafter, in the experience I cite, the church grew in wisdom and in stature, and at least in some favor with man, it continued to be limited in its progress and witness to the perception of the slowest-moving elder. For that neighborhood, in those spiritually demanding and morally strenuous circumstances, that pace was not enough. Had the church incubated for five or eight or ten years, preparing for witness in a serious way, developing its core of ministers of the gospel, and proclaiming its stand only from the basis of Biblical enlightenment and experienced observation, then the impact would have been greater.

In the old, established, century-old parish I now serve, with its thousand-plus members and its large list of distinguished officers and leaders, it would be considerably easier to diminish the size of the rather large governing board to the small handful who would exhibit (and who, verily, already have exhibited) willingness to undergo any discipline that gives honor and glory to our Lord, and thereby sharpen the witness, eventually broaden the service, of the church.

A frank facing of factor Beta does not need to inhibit the institutional impetus of the church; rather, it would give honest expression to what most people know already.

One week-night, when I was sitting in the house of God, I was not thinking much about the preacher's sermon, for I did not believe it. The thought struck me, "How did you come to be a Christian?" I sought the Lord. "But how did you come to seek the Lord?" The truth flashed across my mind in a moment —I should not have sought Him unless there had been some previous influence in my mind to make me seek Him. I prayed, thought I; but then I asked myself, "How came I to pray?" I was induced to pray by reading the Scriptures. "How came I to read the Scriptures?" I did read them; but what led me to do so? Then, in a moment, I saw that God was at the bottom of it all, and that He was the Author of my faith; and so the whole doctrine of grace opened up to me, and from that doctrine I have not departed to this day, and I desire to make this my constant confession, "I ascribe my change wholly to God."

The Autobiography of Charles H. Spurgeon, Vol. I, p. 169 (quoted by Leo K. Brown, *op. cit.*, pp. 59–60)

V

WHAT HAPPENED
TO CONVERSION?

Thus far we have not even discussed conversion as a membership standard, thereby undoubtedly paining those to whom it must be the crucial element in entering the church. Is it not the most valid of measurements for being a Christian? Would it not possibly cut the Gordian knot of having any criteria at all?

Ever since liberal theology crept into the attitudes of the Protestant Church, we have had a dilemma on our hands in the matter of conversion. Whereas, heretofore conversion was the accepted manner of entrance for an adult into the Christian faith, accompanied always by a standard acceptable set of emotional circumstances, the more sophisticated approach with its desire for rationalization at every step almost obviated the necessity of the former pattern of conversion. The leaders of the liberal movement graciously made way for the previous formula to be acceptable, adding to it one or two other alternatives, and giving the name "conversion" to the entire inclusive category. It was generally felt that the manner of entrance for any person to a vital faith was by way of conversion, but the general use of the term was applied to so many different activities of the human soul that a confusion was begun that exists to this day.

Any study of conversion must, of course, begin with definitions, then continue with descriptions, and finish with analysis. This must be done before any use of the term with meaning and cohesion can be made. It is my intention here to begin with a brief analysis of the standard interpretations of conversion, and then to discuss the place of conversion in the life of the church.

Let us first build a working definition of this term. J. B. Pratt says, "Now as I understand it, the essential thing about conversion is just the unification of character, the achievement of a new self."[25] Wayne Oates calls conversion a "crisis in which the pastor serves as a minister of reconciliation between an adult and God."[26] Blanche Carrier, continuing Pratt's idea, adds: "But the really important and only essential part of it is just new birth by which a man ceases to be a mere psychological thing or divided self and becomes a unified being with a definite direction under the guidance of a group of consistent and harmonious purposes."[27] Pratt adds later, in review of an example of a conversion he sets forth, that the pattern is somewhat standard, as he says, "The process was gradual, the discovery of its finished work sudden, the unification of character brought about was complete."[28]

More and more quotations could be made, generally substantiating this standard theme: conversion is a rediscovery of the uniting forces of character, in reference to the demanding will of God, and is accompanied by the surrender of self-directed forces within. This definition seems to me the surface of both theology and phenomenological psychology. However, for the inquiring mind it does not yet give a definitive understanding, at least as far as I am concerned.

To me, conversion is the dynamic discovery of God's directive, compulsive action to redeem in the framework of the human tragedy, especially made manifest in the self. A conversion evidently delves so deeply into the fundamental basis of human character, manipulating the heretofore unmanipulatable forces of control latent there, that it must be bigger and more profound than its observable results. Conversion must actually have something to do with rebirth, other than the altering of surface symbols. If this is true, then we have been irreverent in evaluating it by those surface symbols, and we have been using the word to refer to many other less profound and less important behaviors of the human pattern.

The most stimulating thought I have come across yet in study on this matter is by Dr. Ian D. Suttie, in his psychiatric analysis of the Master's temptations in the wilderness as a conversion experience:

Each of the three temptations then appeared to me to be a parable illustrating and "exposing" a corresponding morbid social goal, though hitherto I had always accepted them as illustrating the rational and conscious adult snares of vanity and self-interest. It is abundantly clear, however, that there is a systematic refusal to seek or to exercise power, as has already been said.[29]

Although the experience of the temptations of our Master in the wilderness has never been widely accepted as his conversion, I agree with Dr. Suttie that many of the dynamics discovered there will guide us in our thinking on conversion in relation to other people. I will, then, use this train of thought to discover a definition usable in the framework of this important term. If we were to courageously assume that the experience of Jesus in the wilderness was in effect a conversion experience, we would note, to follow Dr. Suttie's line of thought, that Jesus passed through the agony of every major psychotic reaction to discover therein the possibilities of life fulfillment. In a way, it might be said that the Master blazed a way for every type of conversion crisis by facing his wilderness experience from the standpoint of human frailty and emotional escape-weakness, therefore making a conversion experience real and available to all types of men. Examining the wilderness experience of the Master in relation to the definition quoted above, we see the possibility that Jesus faced his discovery of life's meaning first in the framework of schizophrenic thought. The incident of turning the loaves into bread, which Dr. Suttie calls the magical power fantasy, is indeed a valid reflection of the way some men try to meet their problems. Since Jesus was in the wilderness for the express purpose of discovering the meaning and purpose of his ministry, and since he was obviously wrapped in considerable indecision, we may assume him to be in conflict.

The dynamics of the conflict we can only guess, but can further assume that they resemble in nature, if not in dimension, the same conflicts through which every person goes in struggling to find meaning. Recognizing that the bigger the conflict, the bigger the forces at play, so also in the Master's life the conflict must have been of staggering proportions. In it most certainly was the memory of his mother's training, the relation to him of her feeling of destiny about him because of his birth story, the moralistic, legalistic, theistic Jewish saturation of his boyhood, the natural yielding any man feels toward certain earthy practices, mixed with a supernormal feeling of fulfillment of need, and his own loneliness at being so unique in character as compared to his other friends. Whether his flight to the wilderness was a pilgrimage toward God, or away from conflict, we can only guess; but because of our own experience in knowing how wonderful we sometimes feel it would be to "get away from it all," we can at least postulate that the second is true. Jesus may, therefore, have gone not so much to seek an answer consciously as to seek simple solitude as release from conflict made more severe by his contact with society. It is safe to proceed on these grounds because human experience has shown that vital conversions often occur when they are not being sought. And, of course, release to get away from society is basically a schizophrenic motive. While in the wilderness Jesus felt the strong call of isolation, of living in a world of his own, of feeling that the need for relationships to other people can best be manipulated by fantasy rather than by reality. I rather imagine that he was very strongly drawn toward this possibility. But there was within him a healthy dynamic that grasped him and brought him to reality to face the situation. In his answer, "Man shall not live by bread alone," he discovered a new realization of an important dimension of life, i.e., life is best faced on its own terms rather than on the terms we would dictate for it.

The second temptation, which was to perform an amazing miracle, may be more correctly interpreted in Dr. Suttie's terms as a "dependency hysteria." This would mean a demonstration to all that the Master lived in a world of special circumstances, in which he was not required to make his own directive choice, nor to be elaborately concerned for his own physical (therefore mental and spiritual) safety. This temptation Jesus also faced in terms of the world rather than in the terms of fantasy, with a simple dismissal that it is wrong to tempt God. In other words, Jesus overcame this temptation by realizing that as a man he must assume the full independent status of his creaturehood. To this extent, then, he prepared the way in his own life for being a positive channel of truth.

The third temptation, to rule the world, is an obvious paranoid tendency, in which the delusion or fantasy of grandeur and power play an apparent part. That Jesus considered this tells us considerable not only about him but about the great potential of this trait of human nature. If the Master in his first perception of self-value feels drawn to carry this tendency to the extreme, i.e., world power, then this is a real factor every man may possibly face to a smaller degree.

That this is a vital consideration in a discussion of conversion is seen by the fact that Jesus returned from the wilderness to his baptism, the public demonstration of the decided direction of his life. He became a disciple of his cousin John, acknowledging the cry, "Repent, for the kingdom of heaven is at hand." This was an obvious demonstration, in the prophetic tradition, of a life-directing decision. It can, then, be said that it *was* his conversion experience.

This removes the discussion of conversion from the category of change from a bad life to a good life, or from sin to salvation, and puts it into the category of conversion from disunity to unity, from indecision to guided decision, from a purposeless understanding that there is a God to a genuine commitment to his way. This, then, further removes conversion from any set pattern to a complete category of its own.

It was said above that conversion is a discovery in the framework of the human tragedy. This would mean that more than the tragedy of sin is involved; the tragedy also of wayward emotions, and destructive desires in the face of frustration, must also be involved. *Just as Jesus went through the entire cycle of tragic possibility, so I believe is such an element also involved in all other human experiences of conversion.* This would mean that consciously to a small degree, but powerfully and unconsciously to a large degree, every individual who has a genuine experience of conversion treads the dangerous cliff and sees the rocks slip under his feet and stares into the gorge of emotional disaster. Then, turning from this void with his feet still on the path, he discovers that the path has a direction. This feeling is substantiated by the genuineness of the conversion itself, by the quality of life that follows it. Only that person who has passed through his own cataclysmic evolution could be prepared to face the future with an unoriginal ability to meet its problems. One of the great Christian leaders of our generation in reviewing his own conversion experience says:

There were psychological conditions which favored the arrival of the spiritually creative moment. But there were no patterns in the mind which prescribed the form of the experience; it came as a complete surprise. There was nothing in my own past which would predict that the event of that momentous day would be what it was. I hardly knew myself as I became in that unforgettable hour. If ever an impact from an objective source was made on this life, it was then. And that impact was not mere circumstance, accidental or contrived. It was not identifiably human, specific or cumulative. I then was certain it was God. Nothing in all the years of study and living since, has corroded that certainty.[30]

There are many evidences of the startling effectiveness of conversion in a life. No study, however, would be complete without some reference to the classic study made by Harold Begbie, many years ago, in which he pointed out: "Conversion is the only means by which a radically bad person can be changed into a radically good person. . . . Whatever we may think of the phenomena itself the fact stands clear . . . that by this thing called conversion men consciously wrong, inferior, and unhappy, become consciously right, superior, and happy.

It does not produce a change but a revolution in character. It does not alter, it creates a new personality."[31] Paul Johnson touches on this truth with a psychological orientation when he suggests that "conversion includes insights won by mutual interpretation, emotional re-education, by living through significant experiences with other persons, a change of perspective in one's attitudes toward himself and others, new motivations to take positive steps toward worthy goals, a discovery of larger resources within and beyond oneself to rise to life's demand with responsible faithfulness. Together these developments may lead to the transformation of personality."[32]

In all current literature, however, the most poignant and meaningful experience related is that of Anton T. Boisen.[33] In relating his own personal religious experience, Dr. Boisen points out how a conflict of his own cleared suddenly at the age of twenty-two, one Easter morning, through what he called a spontaneous experience. Although he later had to go through severe psychotic reactions, almost to the complete destruction of life values, he attributes to the directive power from his first conversion the direction that carried him through his difficulties. He says, in commenting on this: "We are thus proceeding on the assumption that the correct contrast is not between the pathological and the normal in religious experience, but between spiritual defeat and spiritual victory."[34] Dr. Boisen here, I am sure, is bringing us closer to the wilderness temptation understanding of the fundamental power of conversion than any other objective and indifferent author has ever been.

It is the very contribution of Boisen that adds to this study the flavor of redemption. Conversion could in many ways be adequately described as a psychological phenomenon except that no explanation is visible for conversion's effect. Conversion could be described as a theological phenomenon, except that its connection to a new ability to decide and act is only dogmatic, not explainable. But Boisen adds the flavor of insight to obvious redemptive action. This strengthens the original thesis that Jesus experienced a review of both the

negative and the positive at his time of conversion, and discovered the positive direction to be his destiny.

It would not be proper for anyone familiar with Scripture
and religious history to discount conversion as of primary
importance to the Christian life. If "liberal" theology has come
to a position of religious experience in which some form of
conversion has no importance, or is included only as a happy
option, then liberal theology is wrong.

However, it appears to be equally erroneous to equate
conversion with entrance into the Christian household, or at
least to limit it to that. All the classic conversion narratives of
both Testaments (could Jacob and the ladder, or Jacob and
the angel, qualify here?) occur in context. The nurturing
religious community has already entered the picture, whether
it be patriarchal Judaism, or the distant rumblings of the
Christian conscience in secular culture. In the cases of both
Jesus and Paul, conversion was the crisis of insight in context,
in which the community (even though hostile, in Paul's case)
had made its witness and offered its fellowship.

Conversion, however it occurs, is undeniably valid and
central. Its greatest potential is *within* the church, not at the
gate. It is, perhaps, what the early church was trying to
symbolize by confirmation (ordination), the gift of the Holy
Spirit, the call to ministry. I simply suggest that we allow for
the miracle of conversion within the context of the life of the
church, and give it the recognition, not of the "second blessing" but the reverent awaiting, it deserves. Conversion *should
not be the requirement* or the evidence for entrance into
membership.

Perhaps the wry remark by the editor of *The Christian
Century* in reviewing Billy Graham's Madison Square Garden
Crusade of 1957, that it appeared to be "Christians bringing
Christians to be converted by Christians" instead of evangelistic outreach, can unwittingly assume some new respecta-
bility. Since Dr. Graham speaks with the house language of
the church, and directs his whole theology toward the inthink-
ing of the religious thought-frames, it may well be that his

greatest effectiveness is intramural, and in the line of this chapter, so should it be!

This calls for a tenor of church life in which the life-changing aspects of conversion, and the emotional responses thereby stimulated, have room to exist. This may be partially suggested in the following chapter on liturgy, and partially answered in the life of a church where true freedom is possible; this would be the freedom to be "self in community." It is an interesting commentary on the ways of religious men to notice that the very practices that brought fresh vitality to one generation so easily become the proscriptions for the next and the legalities of the third. Christian history glitters with the precious jewels of conversion stories within the church, which have been frozen by the glare of tradition into patterns of necessity. Even now, sophisticated Protestantism is suffering resurgent embarrassment over the sentiments of conversion and is rendered incapable of discussing it objectively. It needs liberation, first from any requirement by the church that it be programmed, and secondly from the door of the church where it doesn't belong. Let it be thrust into the milieu of Christian worship, service, fellowship, and social action, and let us look with respect upon one another when the Holy Spirit chooses to convert!

"Amen!"

What a thrill to hear this great word ripple over the surface of our congregation at prayer. It is an indication that our worship is an active event in many people's lives, here assembled. Amen! Freely translated, that word means "I heartily agree"; sort of a verbal signature to a spoken petition. It isn't the minister's word; he shouldn't have to say it; the congregation properly responds by saying, yea, shouting the word when the prayer has rightly expressed our common inner yearning.

Worship in the Year of the Person is the family activity of worshiping persons. We become a congregation in our beautiful house of prayer, not an "audience." We all participate in our several roles, each contributing to the "beauty of holiness" in our own way. Sing the hymns from your heart; be musically accurate if you can—if you can't, sing anyway. Read the Psalter with feeling; shout or whisper as the text may suggest. React to the sermon, with favor or resistance, but react. And pray—in the silences and in the music; pray with the pastor or in parallel. And sign your name. AMEN.

Please, help me prepare a prayer for all of us. (The style of prayer we use is called "the collect," meaning that it is the minister's responsibility to "collect" the genuine concern of the people and express it in one paragraph.) I need your counsel in my "collection." As you know, I draw freely, and with great appreciation, on the classic prayer literature of the church for centuries back. Yet, in the midst of this experienced phrase-

ology there must be the accent of our own day. Here's where I need your help.

Specifically, let us compose Prayers of Confession. You have often prayed with me my most recent one:

"Prayer of Confession

"Almighty God, before whom we come not because we are worthy, but because we have been invited, we pray Thy gracious judgment upon us. Help us to sense the tragedy in our ingratitude. Lead us to see how deeply we have hurt Thee by living as though the world did not need our concern. Forgive us for making graven images of money, prestige, and expediency, and falling down before them. We love Thee, and we ask Thee to reconcile us to each other and to Thee, and to grant us courage to love Thee, and our neighbor as ourselves. Through Jesus Christ our Lord. Amen."

A Prayer of Confession should genuinely open before God our real, troubled sense of awkwardness, separation, and moral embarrassment. It must be offered in both frankness and faith, for it opens that wondrous gate to forgiveness and release beyond description, the fundamental to all worship.

Write, and send them in. Worry not about literary style. Just open your heart, let the confession flow (it may bless many others) and see if your troubled heart wants to shout out: "AMEN!"

From "The Pastor's Column," in
the *Kirk Journal*

VI

FRUITS OF THE SPIRIT:
1. LITURGY

It is rather exciting to dream about what the church could be, and *almost is*. With its vast contacts, its thousands of houses of worship, its monumental total investment, and its historical imperatives to vital leadership, *now* is the time for greatness! The "givers" are all in place, with the promise of the Holy Spirit who pours out his love upon the church. The life of a particular congregation only awaits a freshened discovery of its own attributes. The heartbeats of a local parish are to be found in the threefold expression of liturgy, Christian nurture, and evangelism.

Liturgy is of first importance to the church, because it is the enactment of basic conviction to the church itself, and to the world. The act of common worship is the existential exposure of whatever the church actually feeds on. If there is any validity, relevance, experience, in the Christian faith, it is evident here or not at all. The church politic is nourished, reassured, rectified, reinforced, here as in no other facet of life. Here is where the current concept of the goals and aims of the church is made manifest, either explicitly or by implication. Therefore, the first focus on the local church must be brought here.

There is no need to use this point to promote certain personal tastes and pleasures in liturgy, which most of us have. Nor does the argument definitely indicate a return to the classical forms of worship. True liturgy can be very contemporary and innovational. Real liturgy (that is, the people's expression) has two fundamental requirements:

1. Christian liturgy requires an *experiential rehearsing* of the *whole gospel* at every meeting. Remember that the earliest liturgies were simple reenactments of the Last Supper and other meaningful scenes. The whole story, and what it revealed about the nature of man before God, was something in which the worshiping community was thoroughly involved as dramatis personae.

A community awareness of the drama of the gospel, its cycle of praise, humiliation, and forgiveness, the acclamation of belief and the privilege of commitment, can be very present in the most simple orders of service. I frequently reflect on the ultraconservative church life of my youth, with its "testimonies," its fervent "Amens," its individualistic bibliolatry, and must admit that it was more honest and liturgical than many of the services I have conducted since. Two decades ago I made a survey by questionnaire of fifty Presbyterian churches in the Western United States, analyzing their liturgical life, that revealed that only about 16 percent of the leadership in those churches even conceived of worship as a community experience. Most of the rationale for worship centered around the gymnasium idea of spiritual setting-up exercises, in no particularly relevant order of occurrence.

Say what you will about the deadliness of ceremonialism, it still functions as a preservative through the dry times. A study of the Mass, in both Roman Catholic and Eastern Orthodox traditions, will reveal a procession of glorious and theologically enlightening events in the expressive life of the congregation which not only touch the intellectual and conscious elements but speak in depth to the symbolic and motivational in ways no younger Christian stream has yet equaled. This is not a plea for the restoration of the Mass, but for meaning in high places.

The nineteenth-century aridity in Protestant worship arose out of the assumption that in the preaching of the gospel, all its parts would be reviewed and experienced. We just happened to pick a century in which the theology of the church was in such strangulation as to be inconsistent, and the preaching reflected the confused scramble for easy answers.

Thus developed the tradition that worship be the exposure of the uncertainties instead of the impressive parade of the gospel. The "folkway" worship of rural Christianity involuntarily became a starvation diet from which the suburban parish (which still unconsciously struggles to resemble the agrarian ethos) has never recovered.

Worship today, then, is the vast largely unexplored frontier, the arena of confrontation of the vital. This leads to the second fundamental requirement:

2. Liturgy rightly expresses what is really there. Like laughter, which is honestly spontaneous, and applause, which is somewhat the same, liturgy is the reflective reaction of the people to the amazing benefits of the gospel. A minister, or lay worship leader, who is in charge of designing an order of worship, is in very nearly the same position as if he had been appointed to organize a rally in honor of the town hero who was intensely popular, and for whom there was widespread genuine gratitude. How best, how appropriately, can these good feelings be expressed in community so that the people have really said what they want to say?

Once again, classical experience has something helpful to offer. One of the earliest kinds of group prayers is the "collect." Here the leader was asked to become aware of the group feeling in any subject such as praise, confession, thanksgiving, or petition, and to "collect" the cream of the congregation's attitude into a very brief prayer, to which those who agreed could vocally consent. Incidentally, in the early church leadership he became, and remained, the bishop, whose sensitivity to the people's major spiritual response was the most accurate.

Many of our present liturgical traditions come out of assumptions that are no longer true. We use the Psalter, assuming that there is enough of a Jewish orientation, or Old Testament flavor, to the church today to make it meaningful. We use long prayers, assuming an attention span in the modern mind which simply isn't there. We even expect the Sacrament of Holy Communion to tell its own story, while in every other part of church life we repress any discussion of the tragedy that the Last Supper reveals.

I quite readily acknowledge that this criterion could develop serious troubles, for many things are "really there" in the worshipers' minds, not all of them worthy. Certainly the exuberance and lightheartedness of the lilting "gospel song" were really there. Certainly the need for assurance, resulting in nineteenth-century Pelagianism and twentieth-century Pealism, is always there. But here again we fall afoul of the "nontheological plus" factors which have to be continually pumped out like bilge water by a disciplined leadership, so that the valid things that are also really there can be expressed. These are a genuine sense of human lostness before God, an actual hunger for the holy, a sense of the majesty, and many kinds of emotional expressions of thanksgiving, as in tears, laughter, drama, even testimonies.

The branch of Christianity called "Protestantism" is starved for a basic symbolism. Any psychologist, anthropologist, or historian understands the great necessity of adequate symbols. Every culture that has thrived and contributed to the welfare of the world, any movement that has fulfilled the need in the lives of men to find purpose, each faith that has seemingly adequately explained the profound foundations of life, has developed a rich symbolism. Because it participated deeply of the quality of its object, it became the essence of core loyalty, wearing deeply into the minds, hearts, and thinking of followers and devotees. This symbolism maintained an inward witness, encouraging those who follow, and an outward witness that informed the world of something of the nature of that symbolized.

Symbols are not invented; they develop. Symbols are neither promotions nor accidents; they are the external evidences of meaningful experiences, felt by large numbers of people over a considerable period of time. A symbol stands for something above language and inexpressible in the common tokens of the day. Writes Lewis Sherrill: "A symbol is a sign pointing beyond itself to something which it represents because associated with it, or participating in it. That which the symbol represents cannot be grasped by the ordinary use of the senses."[35] Continuing a list of other definitions and modifications, Dr. Sherrill comments:

A symbol is not arbitrarily chosen to represent that to which it refers. Rather it is inwardly and organically related to that to which it refers. This means that the symbol is rooted in some historical situation, or event, or in something so familiar to people as to be a matter of common knowledge. This further means that the symbol is rooted in a community, that it carries undertones and overtones of meaning, and that it can be used as a means of communication in the community where it has its roots.[36]

A symbol is more than an imparter of a message, or the carrier of a complete thought. A word or a sentence can carry a message. A symbol, at least in the sense we are now using it, carries more than a message; it carries a combined cultus of experience, and an emotional content of feeling and attitude. Since that which symbols signify in human life is considerably beyond language or any form of articulate expression, we find ourselves completely in the area of feeling.

We see, then, that a symbol is more than a historical footprint, vestige of dead experiences, but rather, it becomes a living and contributing part of the life of the community that produced it. Further, the continuing life and quality of that community bear a direct relation to the meaningful places in its common life of its own most qualitative symbols.

The several portions of the mainstream movement known as Christianity have developed many widely varied, meaningful symbols, which to this day express a fullness, belongingness, and richness that can never otherwise be set forth. The truth of the self-sacrificing nature of a loving God, as expressed in the symbolism of the lamb slain for the remission of sins, the symbol of God incarnate in the form of a suffering servant, God's redemptive love as seen in Christ's sacrifice on the cross, and the truth of the redeemed family of God as symbolized in the rite of Holy Communion are all seen as profound contributions to human culture that reach deeply into the psychic roots of man's ability to appreciate the nature and origin of life.

For example, we turn especially to the symbol known in Christianity as the Apostles' Creed. Like so many other great symbols in any tradition, this creed was the result of controversy and high feelings. It emerged in a period of strife, in which the church was attempting to precipitate and solidify its basic understandings of its own nature, and at the same time formulate its own correctives to the moribund secular thought of the first three centuries. Beset on all sides by opposition and by diverse opinions as to the meaning of Christ and the gospel, the infant church struggled to maintain its own Scriptural and historical integrity by asserting itself in statements of faith and purpose.

In particular, an answer was needed to the enthusiastic but heretical efforts of Marcion, ca. A.D. 180, who in trying to reform the church and bring it to what in his opinion was the true meaning of the gospel, led many of the church dangerously close to the Gnostic heresy. To Marcion, Paul was the only apostle who had understood the gospel. All the rest had fallen into the errors of Judaism. The God of the Old Testament is a just God, in the sense of "an eye for an eye and a tooth for a tooth." He created the world and gave the Jewish law. Christ, who was a Docetic manifestation, revealed the heretofore unknown good God of Mercy. God of the Old Testament opposed him; but in Christ, the authority of the Jewish law was done away, and the "just God" became unjust because of this unwarranted hostility to the revealer of the "good God." The Old Testament and its God are therefore to be rejected by Christians. Christ proclaimed the gospel of love and of righteousness by faith, though, curiously enough, Marcion was extremely ascetic in his conception of the Christian life.

Not only were the Patristic fathers concerned that this error receive a proper answer, but they were guided by a keen understanding of the very values that would keep a newborn tradition such as Christianity vital through the years. R. G. Collingwood assures us that it was their diagnosis that "the 'pagan' world died because of its own failure to keep alive its own fundamental convictions."[37] Further, they presumed to understand why this failure, i.e., that in metaphysical error, the pagan world had become confused as to what these convictions were. The remedy, therefore, was a more accurate metaphysical analysis and its expression in the common life of the influential culture. The new analysis they proposed was what they called the "Catholic Faith," in which the basic presuppositions were a belief in God the Father ("There is a world of nature which is always and indivisibly one world"), a belief in God the Son ("This natural world is nevertheless a multiplicity of natural realms"), and a belief in the Holy Spirit ("It is a world not only of things, but of events or movements"). This Catholic Faith was essential to salvation. According to the late Dr. Collingwood, this was a metaphysically correct analysis.[38]

It was from this need and turmoil that the Apostles' Creed was born. Not the invention of one man or council, nor the careful and deliberate proposition of a select group of theologians, but rather, the emergent common voice of a church eager to state its faith in purity, clarity, and simplicity, the creed was the result of the community's struggling to find, and in actuality discovering, a meaningful symbol to preserve the faith of the present, and to present it in clear form to the future. Its early form read:

I believe in God the Father Almighty; and in Jesus Christ, His only begotten Son, our Lord, who was born of the Holy Spirit and the Virgin Mary, crucified under Pontius Pilate and buried; the third day He rose from the dead, ascended into the heavens, being seated at the right hand of the Father, whence He shall come to judge the living and the dead; and in the Holy Spirit, holy church, forgiveness of sins, resurrection of the flesh.

The fact that it has remained a central symbol of the orthodox faith for every main branch of the church affirms its continuing fulfillment of its basic intent, and its genuine value as a symbol. As the years of practice and tradition went by, however, the church's traditions became deeply involved in lesser and inadequate symbols, until there was a confusion not only of the symbolism but of the purpose of the faith. The Protestant Reformation, in attempting to deal realistically with the corruptions of history, unintentionally also dispensed with a reliance on symbols that had kept the church so consistently intent on performing a mission in history. Protestantism, then, has tried too long to present its case to the world in word and act, and in overlooking and bypassing the creative use of symbols, made its own task that much harder, and nearly self-defeating.

That the Apostles' Creed as a symbol of central meaning in Christian faith and life carries great potential is amply demonstrated in many pastoral experiences. Upon coming to a young, active, enthusiastic, but not too highly informed, congregation, one young pastor introduced the frequent use of the Apostles' Creed as an act of worship, only to find that for the majority of the people it was a completely new and unknown innovation. Without the prestige of historical usage understood, this creed immediately became a focal center, a screen on which to project present needs, tensions, and anxieties. There were three distinct stages of adjustment through which the congregation passed in reaction to the creed.

The immediate interpretation developed along social lines. Practically instantaneously, a fissure appeared between two groups—what the psychologist might call the ingroup and the outgroup. The ingroup, it appears, was made up mostly of charter members of the church who had worked together at great personal effort and sacrifice to bring the church into existence only five years previously. The outgroup were mostly people who had come into the church within the past three years with a "corrective" motive, to straighten up the "questionable (liberal) theology" of the founding circle. It was this second group that pounced upon the Apostles' Creed as a measure of "orthodoxy," proclaiming it with vigor, nearly shouting it in church, and giving accusatory sidelong glances at members of the ingroup who were either cautious or non-cooperative in the use of the creed. It was the first group who approached it with the more open mind, asking relevant questions, taking much time to research and understand, receiving answers in fairness and appreciation.

In effect, this first reaction stage had nothing to do with the creed or its contents, but rather displayed only a deep-felt division already present, in which the creed was used as an instrument to emphasize an emotional difference and to express a social hurt. It is worthy of note that those who clung most loyally to the use of the creed were the least secure in their social situations. So, the creed immediately became a stimulus. Again, as in the days of its origin, it was involved in conflict and struggle. However, instead of this conflict being over doctrinal suppositions, and basic meaning of the gospel, the meaning appeared along lines of the division that was in fact already there, but unidentified, of psychological security and group status.

At this point the entire congregation, under the leadership of the pastor, launched upon a study of the creed and its meaning. The second stage appeared as one of transition. The previous lines of division began to be quite blurred, and eventually became quite invisible. Still, without much in the way of doctrinal meaning, it disappeared as a measure of intergroup division, and came to be a part of the common life of the congregation, in which many felt belongingness on a personal basis, in varying degrees.

But the third stage came into being, and lines of demarcation again appeared, this time completely different. This was where personal and inner feelings became apparent. Those who were seeking reasons to be anxious found them in plenty in the creed. Tokens of exclusion were discovered in each paragraph. "I cannot accept this phrase, therefore I cannot be one of the church." In most cases, thorough pastoral examination revealed that the doctrinal difference was minimal, but the emotional need turned up by the incident was deserving of immediate attention from the church and other therapeutic sources.

It is in this third stage that the church now finds itself. It will be many years of instruction and use before the creed becomes an accepted and central symbol in the life of this particular church, but in the interim, not only is its developmental life touching deeply the doctrinal and subject matter of the gospel in which the church lives, but also it is making considerable and significant effect upon the sociological and emotional needs of the church as a worshiping community. It happens to be this writer's opinion that the whole process is beneficial, and in the long run, therapeutic. The creed fills its purpose as a symbol when it touches people and troubles them at their more profound and otherwise unreachable levels. As a feeling of connection with the past, and as its experience grows, the congregation is discovering a better underlying security and purpose. Some few people who are now emerging as spiritual leaders in the congregation (from both groups discussed above) now affirm that the creed is a very helpful act of worship and declaration of faith.

This experience in the life of one congregation reveals the symbol-starvation that Protestantism unknowingly inflicts upon its people. The historical symbols offer a vast opportunity for drawing out, identifying, and rightly helping those twentieth-century problems which are indeed related to the first and second centuries as well. Bred in one kind of controversy, and found to be an adequate expression of a community answer, these symbols have much to say to the struggles and problems of all ages, because of their antiquity, message, and place in common experience.

As has been said, symbols are not invented, they emerge. One wonders whether in modern-day Protestantism a more accurate symbol would not be the typewriter, the pledge card, or the committee calendar, rather than the cross, or the traditional forms of architecture, or orders of worship and statements of faith. By refusing to meet and recognize the right use of adequate symbols given to us by the past, we have forced (or manipulated) the development and use of low-level and unworthy ones.

Symbols cannot be promoted. No one man or committee could direct the church into a right use of meaningful symbols. Therefore, when the community discovers its real heritage of symbolism, it will be a rich, well-sustained, and emotionally strong community. When it has to rely on its meager experience of the present, a shallow knowledge of the past, and a weakness of understanding of its tradition, the emerging symbols will be those of desperation and mediocrity, and in quality far below the great meaning of such symbols as the Apostles' Creed.

To repeat: liturgy in the church has two functions: to rehearse, thereby to remind, at least, or even to reexperience the gospel in all its revelations, and to provide a genuine channel of expression of the real. When these two are true, the church is at least dealing with the right subject matter.

The education in the schools brought no emancipation but rather reinforced the training of the home. In the elementary schools the children were instructed in sacred song. They learned by heart the Sanctus, *the* Benedictus, *the* Agnus Dei, *and the* Confiteor. *They were trained to sing psalms and hymns. How Luther loved the* Magnificat! *They attended masses and vespers, and took part in the colorful processions of the holy days. Each town in which Luther went to school was full of churches and monasteries. Everywhere it was the same: steeples, spires, cloisters, priests, monks of the various orders, collections of relics, ringing of bells, proclaiming of indulgences, religious processions, cures at shrines. . . . The studies all impinged on theology, and the Master's degree for which Luther was preparing for the law could have equipped him equally for the cloth. The entire training of home, school, and university was designed to instill fear of God and reverence for the Church.*

Roland H. Bainton, *Here I Stand*
(Abingdon Press, 1950), p. 27

VII

FRUITS OF THE SPIRIT:
2. CHRISTIAN NURTURE

Christian nurture is the second arena of defeat or survival. This is also the place of more heat than light, more activity with less effectiveness, more feeling than producing. In effect, in all branches of the church, this area is sheer chaos.

We don't need to rehearse the different theories and directions this discussion has gone through in the last half century: how we have tried to be effective through promotional innovations in Sunday school, tried parochial schools, released time, daily vacation church schools; how we have transplanted the circle of first responsibility from the church school teachers to the church boards to homes (the Presbyterian "new" curriculum of 1948, still untried); and now our swooning intoxication with adult study groups. We still remain 90 percent ineffective in interpreting our purpose to one another, and our content to our own leaders, let alone saying anything of prophetic relevance to the world.

So I come, as you knew I would, back to factor Beta, our little, ignored villain in the piece. We have never really stopped to single out the elementary problem of who is teaching what to whom. We have had no disciplinary voice raised to indicate just why we should be teaching, and who it is that *must* be taught (as over against those who may be taught) that the integrity of the church and the purity of the gospel be honored. Overlooking Beta, we have said that any conversation in the nave was good so long as it was sincere, and we could teach the gospel properly by *being* God's people as well as talking about it. And so, like an organism suffering from an interior infection, we have wondered for years at how the outside world could pollute us so badly, when we were practicing no effective hygiene; that is, identifying and isolating the poor theology within.

This is meant to be no indictment at all of the Christian educator, from the nursery assistant to the dizzy heights of the denominational headquarters, for these are the very folk whose noble struggles should be either validated or declared mercifully surplus. As a matter of fact, outstanding names in this field, such as Lewis Sherrill, James D. Smart, George L. Hunt, Randolph Crump Miller, and of course, John Fry, have been more courageous than the professional theologians in facing the actualities of contemporary Christianity. We are now at an opportune way station. Our noble experiment to make of the family circle the vital heart of the church's reproductive process was at least financially successful, so we can retire it in honor. Besides, Fairchild and Wynn have rather convincingly shown us that the family is a derivative unit of the church, and cannot be used as an originator of values or as a basic educator. So now the responsibility bounces back, for the third time in a half century, on the church (having tried to shunt the burden onto the public schools, then to the DCE complex).

But enough of the critique. To me, unlimited possibilities for the recovering of the fumble are to be found in proper use of the insight of factor Beta. Some pedagogical maxims first: (a) the church must teach or die, thanks to Paul Calvin Payne, William Jennings Bryan, or Horace Bushnell, or whoever said it first. Obviously, the church *has* been teaching, for it is still alive, if that's the proper term to use. (b) Teaching has two dimensions: the imparting of content and an interpersonal relationship of many unspoken meanings. (c) Teaching, to be effective, ought to be done by those who both know the content of the gospel and are involved in its subjective references. (d) What is taught should both derive from, and give support to, the liturgy. (e) Just as a working understanding of the multiplication table underlies any use of mathematics, so must the Bible be the basic talking point of Christian education; and just as calculus is the physicist's working tool, so are systematic theology and the creeds of the church the basic language on which educational involvements are built.

All these are elementary and rather nonstartling. Add to them the thesis of this opus, and some other less happy dimensions appear.

It is an underlying supposition that Biblical theology is only rightly represented in the processes of Christian nurture when it becomes the framework of a personal experience, rather than a resource for a body of knowledge. As I have come to see it, we are trying to outgrow an old concept that the Bible is a flavor book for the teaching of moral and theological precepts, and embrace the understanding that it invites us to participate in an eternal and timeless drama of redemption.

To this end, I shall set forth, in necessarily skeleton and too-simplified form, my impressions of this new notion, especially as an example, in relation to those in the twelve-to-fifteen-year-old group, known as junior highs or intermediates. Since this is the age of confirmation, we focus on it as the principal target group of Christian nurture.

1. Where Is a Junior High? He is between heaven and hell, between infancy and adulthood, between bewilderment and confidence, and between profound isolation and simple faith. If any age truly represented the "belong nowhereness" of life, this is it. Feeling ready to abandon the obviously outgrown modes of childhood, but not *really* wanting to, the early adolescent stands most clearly in the place of opportunity to the Biblical understanding of covenant. At this age, there remains a vestige of the pure curiosity of childhood, but it is beginning to be fused with the emotional necessities of new adjustment, which means that this person will have strong, but only vaguely definable (and answerable), curiosities in certain directions only. Almost all of these will come in the area of relationships. Some of these follow:

First, the matter of social relationships as they apply to groups is important. The developing youth has not yet found an answer, or even a hypothesis, to the question, Who am I? There is a deep need to feel that somehow the reply to this will assert that he is a person of value, but so far in life he hasn't quite found out how or why. So he looks carefully at his relationships to the group, the gang, the "guys," to see, mirrored in their eyes, a value judgment. There is so much innate anxiety behind this quest that it is accompanied with a genuine fear of being found wanting. So there is the conflict of "need to conform" against the natural expression of individuality shown in nonconformity. To be identified as one of the group is as essential to adolescent security as food and drink; to be approved as "one of them" is that which there is no thanwhicher. Yet, in this very acceptance, there rumbles the fear that something has been sold short, namely, the quality of uniqueness. This latter later comes to the fore to claim its own in the developing person, but at this age is only the root of an unidentifiable conflict.

The early teen-ager, then, is happiest when he is one of the crowd, but not completely happy. He is glad to surrender his moral judgment and discrimination to the will of the group, and offer this to society and history as the most valid of all reasons for doing anything, but yet will feel aware within that he ought to be more than that. This is the first of his several causes for guilt feeling.

Some of the best group experiences in the whole growth ladder can take place at this age, because the "groupness" frame of reference, the desire for recognition and acceptance, and the fear of "going it alone" are so strong. Both worship and recreation become experiences of "the body," in which the full participation of the surrendered teen-ager is an observable phenomenon. Yet, at all times, the junior high has only "loaned himself out," temporarily, to this kind of thing, feeling down deep that the time for his becoming a distinct individual is yet to come, and will, by George, when he gets up enough nerve.

Second, we find the area of relationship to particular persons significant. This is the age of hero worship, crushes, and buddies. Like a man learning to walk, the adolescent has to find his crutches, both in reality and in fantasy (and the difference between the two is hazy and not at all important). These usually appear in the form of individuals upon whom the youngster becomes quite dependent for a time. In the case of hero worship, an adult becomes either a parent substitute (because the real parent had, of necessity, to be rejected), or fulfills an idealistic fantasy venture, so necessary to this age. It is not easy for the adolescent to become disillusioned with his hero, because he will simply refuse to believe reality when it conflicts with the dream. Besides, it is the dream he needs and uses, not reality.

The teen-ager chooses special friends as buddies, simply because he must have, somewhere in his environment, some peer who uncritically accepts and supports him. This is as necessary to his emotional growth as the tie is to the railroad. If there were not this pocket of recognition in the world of hostile adults and indifferent peers, life would be unbearable.

So we see that the early adolescent uses all his single relationships as ego-supporters, not necessarily to learn the truth about himself (as in his relation to groups) but to gird him up to produce an as yet inadequate confidence in being.

Third, we now turn to the developing sexual awareness. Our culture is excessively clumsy in handling the preparation for this (usually reacting against the way a previous generation bungled the job), but perhaps this whole step has its greatest meaning in the framework of conflict and discomfort, rather than an easy and unnoticed evolution. The biological changes are near-traumatic at this age and produce, even in the best of situations, violent results.

Yeaxlee rightly points out[39] the undebatable connection between the physical development and necessary emotional understanding and adjustment. Adults tend to underemphasize, or deliberately (even embarrassedly) overlook, the change in world view and life perspective brought about by the new adventure of sex ability. Although we could go on for pages about the problem of sex difference and differential in maturing ages between boys and girls, and what this does to the adolescent society, and also about the special anxieties created in the lives of those "left behind" by either physical development or the social graces, we can cut the Gordian knot by saying that the emergence of interest in sex is the birth cry of the emergence of the self. He is not only becoming a man, he is also becoming man. She is not only an attractive, desirable, and capable sex object, she is woman. This is a special, personal ministry from some unknown beneficent planner who has obviously taken pity on a valueless and ordinary child and ordained him into a person.

This picture is the most highly colored step in growth. There is the facet of guilt, as new standards become necessary, and new drives force early innocence into irrelevance. There is the willingness to accept the invitation to become an adult and join the human race, as opposed to the equally strong desire to crawl back into the womb and become a disentangled spectator. There is a high excitement and feeling of destiny, and an acute conviction of inadequacy and fear of being found out.

Sympathetic understanding and cooperation on the part of adults is desirable, but by no means the complete answer. An adult is a foreign animal who, though helpful at times, is completely divested of any ability to know or understand the adolescent conflict. He is to be respected, obeyed, and tolerated, but never permitted into the inner sanctum of the arena of personal conflict, for he would find too much to criticize. An example of adult cooperation at its best occurred in my parish not so long ago. The mother of a thirteen-year-old boy, in cleaning the house, found evidence that the boy had been using towels for secret masturbation. She removed the towels, and put a box of Kleenex by his bed with the note, "Please use these." Not understanding, the boy again used the towel, so one day it came to conversation. The mother, who seemed most casual and unalarmed, said: "Johnny, your father and I know you are growing up, and that you need to play with yourself. Your father and I have talked about it and have come to a conclusion: please use the Kleenex, we need the towels."

There was laughter, and complete acceptance. Later he thanked his mother and made a feeble attempt at praising her. He didn't really think she understood, or even that his father did, but he appreciated her accepting attitude. What might have been an incident of estrangement and rejection turned to another necessary recognition of his value as a person and a member of the family.

A few summarizing principles about this age could be put this way: the junior high is ready to assume many consciously adult characteristics, but is so tender he could be easily side-tracked. He has to be coaxed out of his hiding place by accepting and approving relationships, to groups and individuals. He has to be encouraged within these relationships, but he must make all his great adjustments alone, under his own power, and guided largely by his own insights. Therefore, the avenue of approach to him is through the relationships he values the most, in forms that seem to be completely foreign to anything representing authority, so that he can pounce on every discovery as his own. He needs to feel, for instance, that his own solution to his mysterious sex tensions and resolutions is the result of his own highly valuable and noteworthy will.

We cannot approach or deal rightly with the matter of guilt at this age, except to say in passing, first, that it is the most significant single dynamic of this age; and second, that it is in the handling of it that the adolescent becomes either a self or retreats from living. For all its exterior handling by accusatory adults or moralistic society, the end result will largely be the indication of the wholesome value of the gang relationship and the adjustment to authority.

2. How Is a Covenant? The foundation stone of Christian teaching is the concept that our God is a Covenant-God. The historical reality of a covenant, vital as it is in Biblical story, is only a symbol of the truth it reveals about God.

In Biblical understanding, a covenant is a published (that is to say, revealed to all parties) agreement between God and his children, in which the terms of their relationship are clearly set forth. According to this revelation, God is no puppet-manager, dangling his creatures on the end of a limiting string, calling all the shots, and making happen in us what he wanted to happen all the time. He grants us the respect and privilege of making choices, and he will even stand by with divine restraint should we choose to clobber our brother and go to hell.

Covenant also says that God is not an indifferent uncle who sends us a small check once a year, but makes no other outward sign of relationship. He is concerned, so much so that he is willing to make actual, visible, historical demonstration of his love for us. "I will be their God, and they shall be my people." (Heb. 8:10.) He enters into our predicaments with personal involvement and injury on his part, and when we lose battles with life, he is hurt.

The covenant is a supreme understanding in human experience because it affirms to us that our participation in it is not dependent upon our quality or actions. We neither earn nor deserve it. The covenant is offered to us with no strings attached, other than our acceptance and enjoyment of it. We inherit our Father's fortune, simply because he is our Father, and we his children, and this is a fact determined long before we could do anything about it. There is neither denial nor disillusionment possible on our part; the covenant is ours.

The basic proposition of the Biblical covenant is so completely different from a natural assumption, or the usual idea of the God-man relationship, that it must be taught. It cannot be assumed, or entrusted to inference. The life of the church must resound with reiterations and reassurances of the nature of the covenant, and what it teaches us about the nature of God. There will be no comprehension of the nature or necessity of redemption, unless we discover to what extent God has involved himself in our predicament. The covenant is an arrangement in which God takes all the risks, yet we tend to think it is we who gamble by entering into a relationship in which we might be judged, condemned, and lose all. Early reactions to religion come from fear of falling short of moralistic requirements and therefore being disqualified for salvation. It is because of this that the proper presentation of the covenant principle is important, and most especially in the life of the adolescent.

3. What Do We Teach? I prefer to face the subject of educational implications of the foregoing in two parts: needs and methods.

a. Needs. The teen-ager needs the covenant. He needs it as an underlying assumption in his whole life. But this statement is too general to handle as it is. It must be analyzed.

The junior high's first need about the covenant is to feel that it is valid. Most of our religious education systems collapse at this point. They become simply content, handed on as though mathematical formulas, without involvement of those handling them. Every point of validity in religion is a point that people are willing to submit themselves to at the vital depths. The teen-ager will never see any personal relevance in the covenant unless he dwells in the midst of a people of the covenant. This paper could end right here on a negative note by simply pointing out that the covenant is not discovered away from God's people, and if a church is not a church but a coasting fragment of Western culture, the educational process will never get off the ground. But the positive side is this: if there are adults who, persuaded of the relevance of the covenant for their own lives, are willing to involve themselves emotionally and intellectually with junior highs on this basis, the process has a good start.

Here factor Beta adds much helpful material. First, there is the already stated principle that this process of Christian education will involve only the confirmed membership of the church. Secondly, this is an extraordinarily fine place for the "apprenticeship" system earlier suggested, in which part of the training for church membership will require necessary involvement as an apprentice with periodic interval changes, to some "lay" Christian who is witnessing to the holy vocation of his common life, not only in church-related, but most especially in the circumstances of his worldly, life. Here the covenant becomes real, for it appears as a continuing experience and an overarching truth into all parts of life. It is given vocal witness within the ranks and associations of the church, but it becomes a realistic and apparent fact of life in the marketplace, on the playground, in the social associations, and at the time of hard chores. When the church insists on disciplined quality among those who would follow the mandates of Christ, the young person is the first to respond with evident admiration, and binding dedication. Conversely, he is all too ready to point out the discrepancies within the church between descriptions of the covenant and widespread experience of its reality. When he can see but a fragment of meaningful loyalty in the adults with whom he associates, he is well on the way toward experiencing the covenant.

The adolescent next must feel that the covenant is relevant, not necessarily in specific and demonstrable terms, but that it is not only true, but true for *me*. Part of the underlying insecurity of this age is the vague suspicion that nobody understands, nobody cares, and God himself has allied himself too much with the adult cause. Put into teen-age terms, the covenant simply means that in the many conflicts and lonely battles, God is "on my side." We need no theological profundity, no doctrinal clarity, here. At this level the truth of the covenant is almost completely emotional and beyond discussion. When, at the mention of the word "God," a youngster pictures a criticizing, rejecting, moralistic authority figure, all the teaching in the world will not help him. But if, conversely, he feels warm, embraced, accepted by a Power that can, then he has the covenant in terms supreme.

Finally, the junior high needs to see evidences of the reality of the covenant in his world. The worshiping community, the church, must be his with a feeling of belongingness. The whole attitude of the church and its leaders toward youth will be significant here. But beyond this is the necessity to see in his secular world, his school, his family, evidence and example that what the covenant says about God is true everywhere. In societies where not too many people claim their covenant heritage, the adolescent must be helped to see what there is, little though it may be.

b. Methods. Here we must obviously operate at a level

considerably different than would be covered by the word
"technique." We deal in emotional growth, subtle response,
accumulation of basic assertions, rather than lesson plans and
room arrangement. I suggest the subjects of acceptance, participation, and induction.

Acceptance is simply that. Whether limited to unspoken
attitude, or made a subject of study, the impression that the
adolescent *as he now is* is an heir to the covenant is important. The leader must somehow impart that God's claim
upon that particular person is the selfsame claim he made on
Thomas or Paul or St. Francis or Schweitzer—*no different,*
and that the leader feels this way too. This is the first law of
adult-adolescent relationships. This is not to imply that no
discipline nor controlling methods be used; in many cases
even strict discipline can be administered without rejecting
the inherent value of the person. This, at any rate, is where
education in the covenant starts.

Participation means that the covenant must become to the
student something in which he finds himself taking part. He
must see in the Biblical story his own predicament rather
amazingly revealed, and then he must find himself swept up
in the consuming promises of the covenant. Whether by
psychodrama, group dynamics, Biblical autobiography ("Write
your life, using the story of Abraham, or Moses, or Paul, as
an outline"), or by simply becoming emotionally involved in
the general teen-age group experience of the covenant, the
child will not grow until he is in it. This means that the old
classroom arrangement of teacher (authority) giving it out to
the quiet, respectful, acquiescent, and receiving students must
be done away with. More to the point is a situation in which
the adult involved becomes himself a part of the struggle,
relating to his own life the same insights, and willing to grow
as he discovers the covenant more. As he consents to this
struggle, he invites his class to join him, noisily putting their
shoulders to the bar, and it becomes a personal matter to
them. When a group will unashamedly discover and admit
that the predicament of mankind in general is one in which

they all share, the individuals within the group will be able to admit their own participation in it, too.

I use induction in the electrical, not the philosophical, sense. Wherever there is a field of electrical current, another can be induced simply by putting a coil or a wire *parallel* to the original field. In this method, we discover that there is, indeed, current in the Bible; that is, that there is process, movement, purpose. We see that the Bible is not so much man's deeds as God's dealings, and that in the care of every life he touches there is an emergent purpose and destiny. Further, we see that Biblical history is in a way a model of the individual's pilgrimage to salvation; that to every one of us occurs the personal experience of creation, covenant, Christ, church, and consummation. As we expose ourselves to this exciting field of spiritual current, we come near enough to have the processes of response stirred up within us. The teenager is highly responsive and excitable, especially when he feels there is any relevance to his own development as an adult.

To get the sensation of current, we must have the understanding of movement. This is the core of the Bible, that it portrays the movement of mankind, at God's gracious direction, from predicament to sonship. It is like standing on a street corner watching a great procession go by, and finally realizing that we should be with them, and that we have been longing to be there all the time. All we need do is step off the curb and join them, and we are personally involved. When the adolescent awakens to realize that the Bible portrays this procession of historical triumph going by him all the time, he is *induced* to join, just as he has always been a part of the gang. Whatever the teaching techniques, and I am confident that we shall develop many more as we go along, they must set up a nearby field of spiritual movement.

We must believe that it is not only possible but absolutely necessary to interpret the Gospel in terms which will bring it closer to the cultures in which up till now it has been generally proclaimed in a Western and therefore foreign form. It is clear that this cannot be done overnight. It is also clear that real risks are involved. But our desire to arrive at a truly adequate communication of the Gospel must be stronger than our fear of syncretism. Where there is a deep loyalty to the revelation, that revelation itself will overcome the hindrances and keep us from falling into the temptation of cheap and false forms of adaptation. The time has come when the "multi-coloured" wisdom of God must express itself in new Asian and African expressions of Christian thought and life.

W. A. Visser 't Hooft, *No Other Name*
(The Westminster Press, 1963), p. 124

VIII

FRUITS OF THE SPIRIT:
3. EVANGELISM

Evangelism is the historical imperative of the church. Its very existence in time, its presence in a neighborhood, are only validated by its ability to speak with its surrounding world in authentic and authoritative terms about the gospel. No conversation, no church.

If apparent opposites could ever be considered twins, in the program of the church, evangelism and social action should be seen as one concern. Though they may come from opposite ends of the theological spectrum in any given church, they yet have the same end: the proclamation of the grace of Jesus Christ to the end that every knee shall bow and every tongue confess him. True, social action acknowledges that certain moral goals may, even must, be attained without necessarily the conversion of all involved; yet, the winning of the lost to Christ can never be absent from any approach the church makes to any sort or condition of man.

If these two kinds of evangelism are ever separated, both deteriorate. What we have called the winning of souls becomes membership recruitment, with emphasis on symbolic formulas, and ineffective nurture; social action becomes a pious form of secular service, or (as in Prohibition) pressure motivated by prejudice and a subtle "our side-ism." The two must always be the single, powerful, undivided thrust of the covenant community into the unregenerate world—mainly to proclaim the majesty of the unbelievable things that are true, and their resultant claims upon us; and, incidentally, to appeal to the secular conscience to right the things that are morally and socially wrong.

Here is precisely where factor Beta looms large. Because of our fuzziness and embarrassment about who really is the church, social crisis only brings agonizing interior conflict, and the interpretation that the church gives the world of prophetic Christianity is seldom as meaty as the concern of our highly motivated non-Christian friends. Pettigrew and Campbell's study of Little Rock in racial crisis tells the story beyond any comment here.

Representation must, continually, be made to the world, at all costs, and to any extent, of the truth of the gospel. But in all integrity, these representations must be made carefully from within the heart of the covenant community, and not be assumptions from the minimum level of traditional Christian virtue. The General Assembly of The United Presbyterian Church U.S.A. makes tacit recognition of factor Beta in its social pronouncements; no one for a moment believes that these heroic statements really derive from the whole life of the whole church; they come instead from a high circle of trained, but not necessarily representative, leadership. That they pass the General Assembly (when they do) is more a tribute to the acceptance of proclamatory leadership than a hearty concurrence. And all this supports the contention that Beta is valid.

It is of the essence of the church to be a prophetic community. Perhaps no other function has brought such agonized resistance and evident discomfort as has this calling. And rightly so, for a single glance at the Old Testament reveals that the prophet's lot was always a hard and lonely one. Further, many prophets themselves saw that their office had been forced upon them; they did not receive it gladly, they fulfilled it with pain; all Biblical prophecies are obviously the result of the forcing of the Holy Spirit, rather than the glad performance of the role by contented men. To say, then, that the church must be a prophetic community is to visit upon it a task, in line with its apostolicity, its oboe-ness, which will neither come easily nor be gladly sought.

To be prophetic in our day and time is a superhuman responsibility, so large that even just our wishing that we were cannot alone be enough to make us truly so. The great need for prophets makes it easy to be a false prophet. Surely history has presented us with a vacuum into which so easily rush our dominant wishes, and our popular assurances, rather than the Word of the Lord. Jeremiah recognized this clearly, telling us that the real prophets who had preceded him had been the prophets who had seen the gloomy clouds of human failure and their historical implications, rather than the easy sayings of peace and happiness. He warned that it is comparatively effortless to prophesy peace, but that kind of prophecy will only be meaningful when it actually produces peace. We can safely assume the contemporaneous value of this warning.

It is altogether too simple today to promise peace. In the first place, the people want peace, so that any kind of prophecy with this tenor is bound to be popular. Secondly, the popular concept of peace is far below the Scriptural and spiritual meaning.

The trap into which so many would-be prophets fall in attempting to proclaim peace is the negative value placed on the word. Commonly, we see peace as either military inactivity between nations, or release from inner personal conflict. It is not prophetic to cry that nations must lay down their swords; this is clearly obvious. It is not prophetic to suggest that there is in religion an outer leadership to a sense of greater well-being; this is only too apparent. So, to interpret peace in these two ways is not necessarily spiritual leadership but merely repeating wanted assurances. For if the nations cease to fight and yet have found no purpose in existing as complementary servants in the onward march of history, where has the prophet's message gone? And if the people find that they can rise in the morning without worry but have no purpose to the day, of what good has the prophet's message been? It is no prophet who proclaims that these ends are peace—it is only he who has found willing ears and a desire to be comforting.

What, then, is the peace that the true prophet proclaims? The answer to this is the profound core of human need, and the thrust of the gospel. For *peace is the personal discovery that the human tragedy is God's anguished concern.* Real peace is that condition of life which makes continuation bearable because God cares and his caring is eternally redemptive in nature. The only peace that the prophet can introduce into the stream of human life is the experiential courage to meet life in all its aspects, because God's purposes are at their clearest there.

The part that makes this message truly prophetic is the demand that the prophet must thrust himself into the process. He must admit his authority as one who can proclaim God's truth because his own life has been dealt with by the same moral absolutes now affecting history. The prophet is one who will not deny that the frustrating blockade of sin has been his own biggest problem, and that his picture of God was seen in the framework of crisis. The prophet then continues to make himself responsible for his message by recognizing that the condemnation of pride also condemns him.

If the prophet is a preacher, he discovers that the prophecy is not easy to preach. When a message becomes easy, it deserves only discarding. It has outgrown its usefulness. The preacher finds that if what is truth to him is to become truth to others, it must be a struggle for him to preach it, and a disturbing stimulant to those who hear, for the real peace of the gospel is not that which we consciously expect. The profound fulfillment of life's deepest need has never been an apparent surface goal in life, easily recognizable from any quarter. It is, rather, the reward of a quest, a discovery made through exploring, in faith and revelation, the many terrible possibilities in life. In this vein, then, the prophet submits himself to the testimonies of history and lets his message speak with its own authority, whether he himself gains status by it or not.

Of disturbing emotional significance are the words used by the Old Testament prophets concerning their message. Moses found it necessary after delivering the Decalogue to withdraw into "the thick darkness where God was" (Ex. 20:21). Many of the other prophets referred to their message as a "burden." Still others spoke of the way that their utterances would be heard by both nation and self as "judgment." These speak of personal pain in the presence of truth.

It is my suggestion that we use great caution in the ready use of the word "prophet," seeing it as a burden too heavy for us to want to bear avocationally. If it is our destiny, let it be so. We can only serve by being messengers of the truth, not by soliciting terms of historic respect.

Whereas in the Old Testament, the covenant community was indeed Israel, it was by no means a prophetic community. Rather, it produced prophets. This doesn't necessarily mean that it tolerated them, even though it may have respected them. It doesn't mean that it enjoyed them, though it did listen to them. It was a community that produced a lonely community within itself. It cannot rightly be said that Israel sat in history as the instrument of God's proclamation; it must rather be said that it was the community that provided the setting in which prophecy could take place. In all Old Testament contexts, prophecy always occurs in the singular, and frequently in spite of the community of Israel rather than because of it.

Yet we have said that the church of Jesus Christ is called to be a prophetic community. This means everything that was seen in Israel and more. It must not only be the community in which prophecy is made possible, and individual prophetic voices are produced and supported, it must also be a community that in itself, and because of its very existence in history, brings the judgment of God's Word upon the world. One can see the historical development of prophecy in the Old Testament as simply being the forerunner, the stage setter, of the eventual time when a whole community would be prophetic in nature.

The world of the twentieth century is a natural recipient of prophetic influence, especially from a community. It has been deeply stung by the collective onslaught of Communism, which bases its strength in the doctrine of community responsiveness; it is in mid-century seeing the effect of the worldwide community of Negroes rise and in a near-single voice demand the justice that traditional Christianity has implied in God's will.

In point of fact, this world seems to be chiefly impressed by communities who are willing to be oriented around an ideal, and to accept the full responsibility for living in the implications of that ideal at whatever cost. It is possibly true that the day of the wide influence of a single prophetic voice has of necessity gone forever, and the great things that are yet to be said will be said by communities whose confrontation with history bears its own message.

Thus the call to the church to be a prophetic community is contemporary and relevant, as well as Biblical. But the excruciating discipline of being that community requires inner strictures and developed disciplines far and away above that which any avenue of the church now seems to reflect. It is not up to us to decide to be a prophetic community; it is the call to the church today to surrender itself to a regimen equal to that usable by the Holy Spirit when he wishes.

A final note must be sounded. The truly prophetic inquiry always climaxes in a feeling of God's grace. Years ago a professor of church polity requested his students to imitate a presbytery. The mock presbytery meeting was held in proper form, the rules were followed point for point, the motions were put through in mercilessly correct fashion. The professor's sad comment was, "Gentlemen, let us not forget that even in the presbytery we must remember the grace of God."

This might well be the prophet's watchword. He never forgets that even in the lonely echoing halls of history, where man's agony is known only in terms of bewilderment, there is God's grace. Here is the supreme high point of prophecy; seeing the stark bleakness of man's sin, and over it like a golden dawn a God whose grace is "sufficient for thee." It is from the polarity of this vision that the prophetic community's message gains peace.

So that if I have truly the testimony of a rectified Conscience, That God hath helped me, it is in both respects; first, That he hath never forsaken me, and then, That he hath never suffered me to forsake my selfe; He hath blessed me with that grace, that I trust in no helpe but his, and with this grace too, That I cannot looke for his helpe, except I helpe my selfe also. God did not helpe heaven and earth to proceed out of nothing in the Creation, for they had no possibility of any disposition towards it; for they had no beeing: But God did helpe the earth to produce grasse, and herbes; for, for that, God had infused a seminall disposition into the earth, which, for all that, it could not have perfected without his farther helpe. . . . So that then, if I will make Gods former working upon me, an argument of his future gracious purposes, as I must acknowledge that God hath done much for me, so I must finde, that I have done what I could, by the benefit of that grace with him; for God promises to be but a helper.

Theodore A. Gill, ed.,
The Sermons of John Donne
(Meridian Books, Inc., 1958), pp. 130–131

IX

A MANIFESTO OF ETHICS

Everybody feels that the church ought to be a character-building institution. Of all places, here is where one should emerge with a keen-edged conscience, a strong feeling of right and wrong, a sense of morality, and become a sterling exemplar. Everybody agrees, from the family that sends its children to Sunday school "so they'll be brought up good people," to J. Edgar Hoover, who sees through a statistical rosiness that the church is somehow a bastion of youthful purity.

After all, if the church doesn't teach morals, who will? Hasn't it always been the privileged possessor of the laws that work? Isn't its main business the production of blameless lives?

Herein lies another of the deep, raw, aching, unhealed wounds of Christian history. All these questions are shallow but relevant, naïve but profound. Outside of the Roman Catholic tradition, no branch of the church has consistently faced the relationship of religion to ethics with any degree of success, and our Roman brethren have been both consistent and responsible, but Scripturally wrong. The church is in the business of ethics, not because it started in that direction at all, but because of the historical accident of a measure of interior control, namely, the sacrament of penance, getting completely out of hand.

It is surprising to see that, in the wake of the behavior-conscious, ethically sensitive, Hebrew tradition, the New Testament appears to have no interest at all in moral issues.

It frankly presents the early church with a starvation diet as far as moral directives are involved. Certainly the weak admonition of the apostle James to "visit orphans and widows" cannot claim to be what he implies, a summation of all the ethics of Christianity. The Sermon on the Mount, examined carefully, provides no methods of discerning right from wrong, or serious sin (mortal) from minor infraction (venial). It just isn't there. As a matter of fact, any serious study of the famous collection of the Master's sayings will certainly amount to a confusion of conflicting ground rules.

The church early became an ethical teacher as a side issue to the proclamation of the gospel. The earliest rules were simply house regulations, relating mostly to conduct within the fellowship while the business of worship or instruction was under way. Little attention was paid to behavior in the outside world *except where it reflected upon the church itself*. When, to everyone's dismayed surprise, there arose discourtesy within the church, followed by bizarre examples of impudence and gross immorality, the church missed the opportunity for colossal greatness. The mature wisdom of the apostle Paul, for instance, in dealing with the homosexuality of the Corinthian fellowship entirely outside the realm of morals, and inside the God-man relationship, might have prevailed and saved the church from ever becoming the custodian of conduct it has found itself to be. But those who came after Paul were less prepared to see the possibilities, and were thus forced into becoming judgmental.

Penance appeared on the scene to preserve the public image of the church. Its real motive had only a secondary purity, therefore, and sank to a level lower yet when it was found to be a convenient method of administrative control, and later, of institutional regularity. The extent to which cruelty and despotism entered into its use and abuse shows how far from really preparing the soul for eternal life penance could become.

But, because of penance, and tradition, and theological shallowness, the church now sits in history as original virtue, from which all aspects of the moral life derive. Unabashedly, lawyers are instructed that the basis of all law in Western culture is the Pentateuch, especially the Ten Commandments, that justice is primarily a religious idea, and that the church in some way is still locked in the ancient pattern of stated wrongs, prescribed punishments, and patterned restorations. The contemporary discussions around penology are a case in point: should they be basically punitive, or therapeutic? No one really knows, because the profession of justice is based on an anthropology few modern lawyers have even heard of.

Meanwhile, back to the church! So everyone wants it to build character, to "put the fear of God" into people, to delineate the good from the bad, to promise rewards and threaten doom, to legislate the moral imponderables, and to direct its thrust toward its main product, namely, human responsibility. Is this its calling?

It is probably best at this point to review the alternatives, both as already practiced in history, and as postulated by the theorists.

1. The Church as Mediator of Judgment and Forgiveness. Obviously, we refer here to the classic position of the Roman Church. One has to begin with an expression of admiration for a system that has continued under staggering odds to hold to its basic tenets. The complicated structures of canon law, the meticulous sobriety of ascending *curiae*, the plethora of exhausting detail and split-hair decisions, all somewhat foreign country to the Protestant, are as impressive as St. Peter's itself in mass and intricacy, for the Roman Church has accepted the responsibility to follow through with the gargantuan task that always follows any assumption of moral authority.

Here the church accepts the role of prescribing the things that are right about life, the things that are wrong, and legislating the degrees of difference into positions of dogma. You cannot just say, "Lying is wrong," and leave it at that. To even have said it is to require that further statements be made as to *how* wrong it is, those conditions which make it less wrong or more wrong, and the consequences, in detail, of lying at all levels. Furthermore, one cannot make this statement with any authoritative integrity without providing some directively clear statement about atoning in equal measure for the wrong. And all this, the Roman Church struggles heroically to accomplish, certainly to the admiration if not the agreement of other Christians.

Earlier, I made the categorical statement that this is wrong, and of course am caught in the same predicament of responsibility as described in the paragraph above. It was an unwitting demonstration of the impossibility of an absolute position, including my own. The remark was made because the early church had no intention of becoming the cosmic referee of the divine legal machinery, and because the redemption of which the gospel assures us has little, if any, relation to "goodness," or rightness, or morality, or behavior, or any such thing.

Nevertheless, this is an area like so many others, in which the traditional image of medieval Catholicism yet prevails in the popular mind, and even though the Reformation rotated around this very point, not only the outside world but most of contemporary Protestant leadership yet think that there is some kind of mysterious moral authority invested in the church, and it ought by all means to be teaching, yea, indoctrinating, the guidelines of Christian living in every breath. Ministers and Sunday school teachers alike are harried by questions on morality, most of which they are far less prepared to answer than a civic leader or social scientist.

This alternative has the one virtue of certainty in it, for which most people are sometimes grateful. Every question gets an answer, and every procedure has its prescribed solution. Every offense has its recompense, and there are ways to clear the conscience and feel relieved. The sense of human alienation is yet so strong, perhaps growing stronger in an age of general anonymity, that any direct answer giving assurance of identity and acceptance will be more readily received than a challenge to be involved in a process.

To this extent, this approach to ethics contributes a real service, and has its gloriously valid place in history. There are those scholars who maintain that the whole structure of morality and sense of individual responsibility can be attributed to the medieval disciplines of Western Christianity. This I will not question; rather, the larger question is posed: Should this have been a function of the church of Jesus Christ?

2. The Church as the Proclaimer of a Moral God. The classic Protestant position this, in which the Reformers continued the idea that the church had specifics to contribute to the moral life but refused either to legislate or to mediate, placing the conscience of man directly next to the chastening and forgiving presence of the Holy Spirit. The ideal obviously was that morality then would be more a matter of individual response, and the church would be the community of those who had responded, and therefore a reservoir of accumulated morality rather than a dispenser of judgment. Small errors could be dealt with in corrective relationships within the church; gross sins would most likely be committed by those outside the church anyway; but for those unfortunate and rare intramural episodes, excommunication, and binding over to the civil authorities, was *de rigueur*. In this wise, Luther was at first naïvely Utopian, then sternly paternalistic; leaning always on the public tone of assumed standards, he exerted discipline in sporadic enraged dismay. It was Calvin, whose careful Augustinian anthropology displayed the real nature of the human problem, who erected a system of churchly discipline carefully calculated to keep the house of God in order. Though in the context of his century many of his conclusions (and the death sentences his system produced) were unseemly, we yet travel, in both churchly and political worlds, on the decision-making apparatus that Calvin saw to be vital to integrity.

It is still the spirit of Protestantism that the moral life is a result of the divine-human encounter. It is the official (if not popular) theology that the church exists to call man into this relationship, not because he is worthy, but because he has been invited. On this basis, any minister could rightly refuse to deal with any modern problem of conduct or ethical decision and confine his teaching to the theological implications, and be on safe ground. "How you express this in your life," he might say to his flock, "is your problem, not mine." Indeed, judging from the fantastically infantile moral stands made by the general run of Protestant anthorities, it would be far more preferable for most ministers to do so.

Yet the very fact that this alternative is not used is its own chief critique. The ethical implications of the gospel, though not prescribed as such in the New Testament, are so overwhelming that no community of faith can long hear without being moved to expression. So, when the church sponsored the Abolitionist movement in the early nineteenth century, it abandoned its traditional Protestant position as "proclaimer" and became in some measure the institutional "doer," and it had to deal with issues of morality. All present social action movements now developing so strongly in American Protestantism are illegitimate children as far as the stated theory of the Reformation goes. And it has not yet been formally supplanted.

The greatest historical disasters in Protestantism have been the moral crusades, confused somehow with divine revelation, against vicissitudes of cultural life. There may have been, for instance, quite rational grounds for the early prejudice against social dancing. Certain communities undoubtedly should have banned this practice because of flagrant local abuse. But for it to have become the paragon of shame it was so widely held to be shows how it became used by intuitively clever but morally inept church leaders, as strategic teaching for uses of power. When we deviate from original stands, we ought to know why.

It has often been said that the Prohibitionist movement was a Protestant-inspired phenomenon. It ought perhaps more correctly to be said that it was a cultural expression that arose most strongly in Protestant sections of the country. Once again, it was a cause that had a benevolent rationale, and was directed toward a symptomatic social problem that needed a solution. Yet its momentum was fed by an entirely unjustifiable, even blasphemous, cry of *"Deus vult,"* in which the church was purified by being used in a righteous act. Perhaps no other single development of the twentieth century has saddened the sophisticated longing for the purity of the church as much. When the Volstead Act was repealed in 1933, the prestige of the church as partaker in a "Noble Experiment" began to wane seriously. It had tied its wagon to the wrong star, and perhaps it should not even try another star.

Yet the purists can stand in the ashes and say that the church wasn't even involved; it just proclaimed the Biblical truth, and this was a sincere, if ill-advised, response. Like most purist stands, however, it isn't wholly realistic. The church, as church, *was* involved, as much as in the Holy Wars of Saxony in Luther's time. Sermons were preached, offerings taken, prayers were solicited, and congregations recruited. Therefore it cannot be said that this alternative has even rightly been tried, or if tried, it hasn't worked. No wonder the world still comes to the church for moral guidance, and no wonder it doesn't always respect the answer! Wryly does Reinhold Niebuhr comment that the miserable performance of Protestant Christianity "is derived from its inclination to invest the relative moral standards of a commercial age with ultimate sanctity by falsely casting the aura of the absolute and transcendent ethic of Jesus upon them." He further remarks that a religion that capitulates to the prejudices of a contemporary age is not very superior to a religion that remains enslaved to the past.[40]

3. The Church as Supporter of a Relativist Ethic. Strange that we should even list this, for certainly no group would ever want to admit to condoning sheer relativism. That word has simply fallen into disrepute. Yet in all honesty, it must be listed because it is being practiced.

Relativism is the stand that there is no really absolute, or even consistent, basic ethical demand. It all depends upon the circumstances, and the person must assume responsibility to act with proper intention. After that, no one is equipped to execute judgment upon him, and his decisions are morally unassailable. Lying is wrong in one place, but probably permissible in another, and preferable in a third.

Somehow, the Reformation position outlined in the second alternative becomes interpreted in the ecclesiastical outback in an incipient relativism. The great enlightenment of the church, as the contemporary layman sees it, is the freedom to make his own moral judgments upon his own rational premises. A neomedievalism nearly appears herewith, obliging God to go along with, and be limited to, the consequences of such decisions. One feels as though he has gone full circle in religious history, and the amoral relativism has brought us again to that day recorded in The Book of Judges when every man did that which was right in his own eyes, and there was no prophet in the land nor was there a king.

Who knows how deeply this is engrained into the fabric of American Protestant thinking? Who knows how profoundly it is the essence of response to the gospel? Who can tell when the freedom of a relativist ethic will open the way for a disciplined demagoguery? One wonders if the present struggle for racial justice in which the Christian voice is an embarrassed squeak is not the preparatory fanfare of historical judgment!

Relativism is rampant in the church because the Reformation failed to put ethics into its proper place. Once lifted out of canonical law, it had to be put in a new system of relationship to religion, as the New Testament had it. But, shrugging off the necessity of dealing with conduct instead of judgment, the church permitted the second alternative to be the whole statement, and we cannot but accept the reality of this third one as the actuality in force.

To review the three alternatives, as stated above, we use hypothetical conversations as demonstrations. The first shows the church as custodian and judge of morals:

WOMAN (*symbolizing the world*): Father, I have sinned. I have committed adultery.

MINISTER (*the voice of the church community*): You have done wrong, my daughter. Your offense is serious, and you stand in danger of eternal retribution.

WOMAN: What shall I do?

MINISTER: Are you truly sorry for your misdeed, and do you seriously intend to lead a new life following the commandments of God?

WOMAN: Yes, I do.

MINISTER: Then you will perform the following devotional functions, and take these prescribed retributory steps.

WOMAN: And if I do?

MINISTER: You will be forgiven and your soul will be safe. And this should teach you never to make this mistake again.

Or:

MAN: Father, I stole some money. But the guy I took it from owed me some anyway, so I think it was all right.

MINISTER: According to canon law, you have done wrong.

MAN: I don't think it's that bad. Maybe it was poor taste to do it, but I don't think it was wrong.

MINISTER: Then you are not sorry?

MAN: Well, not as much as you think I should be.

MINISTER: Then I cannot give you assurance of forgiveness.

MAN: And what does that mean?

MINISTER: You cannot have full standing in the church, and your soul is in danger of hellfire.

Now a couple of imaginary examples from the second option, the classical Protestant idea of individual responsibility before God:

WOMAN: Reverend, I guess I've done a terrible sin. I have committed adultery.

MINISTER: Yes, go on. Please tell me all the details.

WOMAN: I really thought I loved him. I still do. But I guess it was wrong to do.

MINISTER: It probably was wrong. What are you going to do?

WOMAN: That's what I came to you to find out. What should I do?

MINISTER: Seek God's forgiveness.

WOMAN: How do I know when I have found it?

MINISTER: I don't know. That's something you'll have to find for yourself.

WOMAN: But do you think I did wrong?

MINISTER: Yes, but it's what you feel about it that matters.

Or:

MAN: Reverend, I think you'll understand this. A guy owed me some money, so I just helped myself out of his wallet.

MINISTER: You stole it?

MAN: I wouldn't say that. I just took what was mine.

MINISTER: Don't you think that's stealing?

MAN: Well, it may be inadvisable. But anyway, now we're even.

MINISTER: What are you going to do about it?

MAN: Nothing. We're even. Are you going to do anything about it?

MINISTER: Of course not. I'm not your judge. It's all on your conscience.

MAN: Good! My conscience can take it.

Now we see the same situations in the light of relativism:

WOMAN: Reverend, I'd like your advice. I have been having sexual relations with a man other than my husband.

MINISTER: Do you love this man? Is it a fulfilling relationship?

WOMAN: Indeed. My husband is a cur, and I've always though I deserved something better.

MINISTER: Possibly you are right. It's not up to me to judge. It looks as though you'd better make an honest woman of yourself.

WOMAN: Yes, I want to divorce my husband right away.

MINISTER: I'll stand by you.

And:

MAN: Boy, did I fix that up! He owed me money, so when he wasn't looking, I took it. Now we're even, and he doesn't even know it!

MINISTER: Pretty clever!

As you review these incomplete and exaggerated fables, you can see that the role of the church changes most radically, whereas the situation of the sinner, though articulated in

different ways, remains the same. The first relationship is
priestly, legalistic, decisive, and complete. The second is
pastoral, realistic, ambivalent, indecisive. The third is amoral,
supportive, evasive. Which of these should reveal the church
in its conversation with the world?

There must be more to say. If there weren't, I certainly
would never have started this chapter. Yet what has to be
said cannot parade under the rubric of a good answer; it may
be just the next step in the church's pilgrimage to ethical
meaning. It certainly does not answer all the problems raised
by the apostasy of the centuries and the need for centralized
guidance in conduct.

The click phrase currently is "contextual ethics," or, to
quote Niebuhr again, his classic title: "The Relevance of an
Impossible Ethical Ideal."[41] Oversimplified, this is the position
that it is the Christian's first responsibility to root himself not
in any ethical imitation of Jesus, but as identified as a target
and relayer of *the love* of Jesus. This puts the Christian immediately into an irreconcilable difficulty of loving the world
that rejected Christ, of being an imperfect vessel of absolute
purity, and of not having the intellectual judgment to match
the requirements of experiencing this love. This means two
things: that the Christian lives under intense discipline of
being loved and aware of this love and its implied judgment,
and then that he is free to act in the light of the love. There
are, in this system, no ground rules of behavior that can be
typified as Christian; there is only dedicated and frequently
fallible response to the ethical demands of the gospel.

The last two hundred years have seen creative, albeit
minority, thinking on the part of certain Christian philoso-
phers whose explorations have brought a new integrity into
the Protestant camp. Existentialism, especially under the influence of Kierkegaard, stresses the threat to Christian faith
and to the unique individual that ensues when ethical principles or philosophical systems presumptuously usurp the
place of the living God. "It also emphasizes the uniqueness of
each situation, and therefore insists that the gospel may have
its sovereign sway and yield its redemptive power only when

it can speak directly and anew to the believer who renounces the false securities of 'rational principles' and who is ready to make unique and critical decisions."[42]

The principle of the uniqueness of the individual and the critical uniqueness of his moral predicaments is discussed, on the sharpest edge, by Niebuhr and our martyred contemporary, Dietrich Bonhoeffer. Here follows an exercise in which we rub these two authors together at coincidental points, to gain the flavor of tandem dialogue. Starting with each writer's basis of his ethical system:

In Bonhoeffer's words:

Formation [of an ethic] comes only by being drawn in into the form of Jesus Christ. It comes only as formation in His likeness, as *conformation* with the unique form of Him who was made man, was crucified, and rose again. . . . It [the Christian ethic] is achieved only when the form of Jesus Christ itself works upon us in such a manner that it moulds our form in its own likeness.[43]

This is a completely strong theocentric ethic. He starts not with the predicament of the world, the needs of society, or moral presuppositions, but with the fact of the incarnation as a revelation to man of what life is all about.

It is essential to note quickly that Bonhoeffer is not limiting himself to any certain aspect of Christ's life or meaning. He fully defends his thesis as the book unfolds. By the incarnation, he means God's saving Word, fully affirming the creation, the love of God, the Fall and its price, the judgment and its answer. Inasmuch as any man can cleave his subjective tastes from his theological judgment, Bonhoeffer has done it, in embracing and presenting an honest Christ-ethic.

Niebuhr's setting is different. He develops his offering in contrast and struggle. He takes the rough shapes of orthodoxy and liberalism, and whittles both down to size by asserting rather strongly what his ethic is not. Instead of centering his view on the incarnation, he uses as his range of vision the Hebrew-Christian world view in which the determining factor is the quality of a transcendent God.

To particularize: Bonhoeffer would use as first reference and final qualification his personal relationship to Jesus Christ in the incarnation and his own response to it. Niebuhr starts with the general framework of prophetic truth, and makes his personal reference to a "sense of depth and experience of tension"[44] this world view imposes. "It is by faith in transcendence," he says "that a profound religion is saved from complete capitulation to the culture of any age, past or present."[45]

Whereas in both systems, the personal relationship is primary, it stands out in much more detail to Bonhoeffer, who keeps returning to the personal experience of the incarnation like a homing pigeon. Since Niebuhr is so interested in the truth of transcendence, his personal relationship is limited to a general placement within the ranks, and an acceptance of the intermediary position of finitehood which is ultimately infinite.

When it comes to attitudes toward the present situations, both men are led to comment. Bonhoeffer, viewing the desperation of those to whom the incarnation means nothing, says:

The most astonishing observation we can make today is that in the face of the void one is prepared to sacrifice anything and everything: one's own judgement, one's human character, and one's neighbour.[46]

In this field Niebuhr is far more profound and vocal, assailing the vain hopes of Shailer Matthews, Frank Buchman, Francis McConnell, and even E. Stanley Jones. Commenting on Jefferson's viewpoint in the *Age of Reason,* Niebuhr writes:

It was wrong in the optimism which assumed that the law of love needed only to be stated persuasively to overcome the selfishness of the human heart.[47]

Both men seem to be quite aware of the dangers of an eviscerated ethic, which tastes of the flavor of Christian culture, but which overlooks the necessity for painful self-involvement. Though each treats this strain with quite different approaches, both steer a skillful and precarious path between Jeffersonian optimism and Kierkegaardian despair. To Bonhoeffer, the supreme (and only) indication of hope is in one's closeness to Christ; to Niebuhr the order of things as seen in the framework of history as expressed in the "love ethic of Jesus" gives life a motive.

Niebuhr's conflict in paradox, which emerges as his climactic affirmation, can be somewhat compared to Bonhoeffer's discussion of the "penultimate" and the "ultimate." Bonhoeffer is here calling us to act, as we are forced to by circumstances, always within the penultimate, or values of immediate and historical consequence, but directed by our personal relation to Jesus Christ, toward the ultimate of his Kingdom. The evident tension of this position resembles, although not exactly, the paradox of Niebuhr.

Love, to Niebuhr, is the Christian's approach to the world and its problems. Love, to Bonhoeffer, is that quality of existence within the community of the church which makes the reality of God apparent to society. "Love," he says, "is always God Himself. Love is always the revelation of God in Jesus Christ."[48] "The mandate of the Church is to proclaim the revelation of God in Jesus Christ."[49] This revelation, Bonhoeffer continues, is manifest in Jesus Christ as the eternal Son with the Father for all eternity, Jesus Christ the crucified Reconciler, and Jesus Christ, the risen and ascended Lord.

What have we discovered in this interscholar discussion? We have posed two great minds in parallel; now we must draw some conclusions.

First, in treating the subject of love, it appears that the main difference between the two writers could be labeled "subjective-objective." Since love, to Bonhoeffer, is the subjective result of a personal relationship, and a personal response to an experience of grace, it becomes an internalization, a quality of living. To Niebuhr, love is the objective inevitable summation of the purpose of history; it becomes the indisputable framework for action. Bonhoeffer finds love as a happy discovery, a divine channel for answering the unutterable gift of grace; Niebuhr sees in love the order of life at its fullest meaning.

Because of this distinction, Bonhoeffer is able to respond with a far more systematized framework of action; he sees all life in terms of its basic mandates: labor, marriage, government, and the church,[50] and these are the divinely ordained arenas for God to speak through his people. Since Niebuhr's God is wholly transcendent, he cannot be "found" in arenas, but only in flavor, or character or prophetic dedication and love, and a "pure" witness is impossible anywhere.

So we see that ethics is a strangely complex field for the Christian. Impossible, and spiritually dangerous, is any system that adjusts the life of the Christian to the life of the world, lest the idolatry of making man comfortable in this alien environment blot out the face of Jesus, who himself didn't fit, yet redeemed. The church will never have the answer to the ethical dilemmas of life; it ought never to claim it does. The church will never have in its message those directives which relieve any individual of his responsibility before God. And yet the church can never give up the ideal of ethical living, and devotion with a moral purpose—thus, the contextual ethic, or the Christian in love with his Lord, giving witness in the world, and doing battle with the forces of destruction, as his faith and his church help him to see them. He acknowledges the temporality of his acts, he confesses that another might judge differently, he realizes the finiteness of his mind. Yet he acts to the glory of God as he can, and commits the result to his Lord.

The meaning of this within the life of the church is either dynamic or chaotic, depending upon local interpretation. But it can only be valid in a religious community of evident discipline. Factor Beta demonstrates that the behavioral conduct of Christians is either within the framework of ethical intentions, or it is outside, in a relative and unstructured ethic of convenience, and at least a line is drawn somewhere.

The church is, indeed, and inescapably, an instrument for action, and the individual members of it as well. Even as

Jesus loved the world, and ministered to it, and died for it, so is the cycle of life for the church. But this means the removal of the whole subject of ethics from the "rules for life" category into the channels of service.

And what about advising the world as to right and wrong? How do we answer the questions of moralistic parents and build the characters of our youth? How can we accomplish this without ground rules? We don't. And the church should be out of that business anyway.

The dimension that has so often been overlooked that the church has to offer is the community of the church itself. What we offer the world is not a code of conduct but a community of concern. We do not propose to fulfill the emptiness in the lives of people by proscription or conduct or list of principles; we simply offer an invitation to be involved with a community of love. We have no predetermined answers to human frailty or racial injustice or international hostility; we just offer ourselves, in the context of the fellowship of those who love the Lord, and the mutuality of our human predicament. And we ask that out of the discipline of worship and the support of fellowship and the conviction of love, answers will arise with meaning. This, evidently, is what the New Testament inferred. "If food is a cause of my brother's falling, I will never eat meat."

Now let us take one more hypothetical run through our fabled interviews, this time assuming the church involved is one that as a community senses the deep life-involving commitment of the love of Christ:

WOMAN: Pastor, I seem to have a domestic and moral problem. I have been romantically involved with another man.

MINISTER: Is it a relationship of honesty?

WOMAN: It is to the extent that he and I are genuine to each other. But in that it involves deception at home, it is wrong, and I cannot continue this way.

MINISTER: What do you feel you should do?

WOMAN: As a Christian, I feel so privileged to know the love of Christ, that I am now prepared to forget my own needs until I have acted responsibly to my children and family.

MINISTER: I assume this means that you will discontinue the relationship?

WOMAN: Possibly, but only if it appears that it would be the only way to retain my faith and integrity.

MINISTER: Then there are alternatives?

WOMAN: I don't know. I hope so. If not, I will do what I have to do.

MINISTER: It sounds pretty difficult. Do you think you can do it?

WOMAN: My friends in the church will uphold me with their prayers. I have often felt encouraged to do the right thing because of them.

MINISTER: If there is a way of keeping this secret love relationship alive while you meet your other obligations, will you continue it?

WOMAN: Yes.

And:

MAN: Pastor, I have righted a wrong. He owed me money, and I took it from him.

MINISTER: Do you feel honestly that it was right for you to do that?

MAN: Well, perhaps it was poor taste.

MINISTER: Is poor taste permissible to you?

MAN: Come to think of it, I don't like the idea. I usually like to do things right. I don't suppose any of the others in the church would do it that way.

MINISTER: How do you think you can rightly show God's love in this situation?

MAN: Well, at least I could have the courtesy to go and talk to him.

MINISTER: I would like to know the outcome.

In traditional terms, neither of these episodes ends in the correction or completion of the problem, and they would therefore be ethically unacceptable. Yet, because in both cases there is the process of reconsideration in the light of God's love and the concerned community of the church, they stand as apt illustrations of ethical power under expression, with creative personal relationships revealed. Morality is always a continuum, in any life, never a series of unrelated victories or defeats. No one incident in any person's experience confirms or rejects him as a moral person. No offense is so light as to be insignificant, or so heinous as to surpass forgiveness; all are part of the mosaic of response to the gospel.

The church, then, teaches Christ. It experiences and radiates love. It acknowledges judgment as life's obvious reality. It lives in a world where behavior is important and, always on the razor's edge of judgment, it lives to the glory of God. And when the choice appears, as it so often does, not between good and evil, but between evil and evil, the church chooses the evil it must, and prays for God to make it redemptive. (A dramatic case in point here is Bonhoeffer's own agonized decision to take part in a secret plot to murder Hitler.)

Let it be made rather strikingly clear that the church expects and provokes ethical living. Let it be accepted that the church attacks the kingdoms of this world to the glory of the Lord. But let it also be admitted that the church is fallible, where its Lord is not, that the church is caught in history, in time, in space, in humanity, in finiteness, and its witness will always be partial and fragmentary. And let the church have such structures of internal life and discipline that occasionally its conduct does indeed reflect to the glory of Jesus Christ, Lord and Master!

God's Covenant is by many dimensions a deeper kind of personal relationship than a contract and must not be confused with any form of bargained pact. In the Covenant of Grace the Church's life is rooted in the mystery of the divine election of a chosen people, and points toward the destiny of human history in God's everlasting Kingdom. Just because this intimate personal bond with God is a gift with promise, it involves a task, i.e., the people's responsible participation in the servant life of God's covenant-community.

Allen O. Miller, in *A Handbook of Christian Theology* (Meridian Books, Inc., 1958), p. 62

X

THE BELOVED FELLOWSHIP

Much is said about the church's being the "fellowship," the *koinōnia,* in which there is a beloved relationship of support and understanding that goes positively unequaled in any other kind of fraternity. That it is such, a community of the chosen, is the basis of romanticized doctrine, but not necessarily a widespread fact. Challenged to "name one" when it comes to confrontations of richer meaning, most local parishes can rise no higher than the monthly potluck "fellowship" dinner, or describe the friendliness of the people at the door on Sunday mornings.

Probably never before in history have so many claimed to have fellowship with so few. Communicant membership displays lists of thousands in each town, yet it is tens who even know each other. The minister rises in the pulpit to announce that "*We* will meet . . . *we* will pray for . . . *we*" when of the assembled worshipers only a handful really intend to partake. This is not to say that there is no such thing as Christian fellowship, it is rather to say that it is not even a living factor in the lives of most who consider themselves Christian.

In point of fact, the word has been used so much to describe what isn't there that it has almost become a travesty on what *is* there. The minister begins his wedding liturgy, "Dearly beloved," and sends most minds into outer space, with hearing aids turned off. The phraseology is not only obsolete, it is incorrect. The church, as it presents itself to the community, is only a vast collection of different people with different motivations, heterogeneous abilities to relate, whose lowest common denominator couldn't care less about getting any more deeply involved with anyone. As a matter of obvious note, the great attraction of the larger church is its possibility of anonymity, its niche of privacy, to which one can repair and then slip away without the inconvenient necessity of being bothered by being known. The subjective reference of Protestantism has unwittingly encouraged the "inner man" to relate to the Holy Spirit as he damn well sees fit, and it's really nobody else's business.

Of course this is an overstatement, as so many are in this work. There are vital relationships in nearly every parish; there is a core of concern, a community of consolation, and the writer's own experience stands high in averring this. But it is also painfully true that this valid *koinōnia* usually derives from the fringe of the church's program rather than from its essence. The fellowship is more accidental than produced, and possibly reflects more the happenstance association of highly motivated and gregarious people than it does the essential nature of the church. To restate this: it is possible that the church attracts the kind of people who can relate in confidence and mutuality, rather than that it points its whole program of interrelationships toward making this fellowship possible among people who were not previously capable of it.

If this is true, then we could tolerate an occasional new thought about fellowship. When a loyal church member, or even leader, who has been in the congregation for years, dies, it is quite a revelation to discover that he has requested a funeral service conducted by his lodge or fraternity "because he had real fellowship there." When a loyal Christian is in trouble, or even disgrace, he frequently turns to outside sources of assistance, too embarrassed to make his plight known to his fellow churchmen, fearing their disapproval.

If fellowship implies a community of healing and consolation, a circle of acceptance and understanding, then the New Testament mandate is for the church to orient its intramural relationships to that end. Emil Brunner, in his little volume of protest, *The Misunderstanding of the Church* (The Westminster Press, 1953), pleads precisely that. Your fondest memory of that beloved Sunday school teacher recalls practically nothing of what he said, but lots of what he was, and how he knew you and loved you. The haunting organ music echoing in the vault of the great cathedral may have stirred your heart to beauty, but it was the warmhearted grocer who stopped at the door to help you that made you go away singing. Could we, then, get along without curricula or vaulted naves? Possibly we could, if the circle of love were as importantly there. Until it is, however, the props will have to stay.

Factor Beta is, you will remember, a contention that the church harbors different kinds of Christians under the erroneous idea that they are all one. Certainly here the truth of the theory is demonstrated, for anyone can draw diagrams of concentric circles and realize they have pictured the "fellowship" of the local church. Once again, the larger number will pertain to the less interested, the outer circle of those whose sense of involvement and participation is minimal. Although they might well be accused of not being interested enough to make themselves known, it can also be said that the church took its own intensity so lightly as to offer very little to get interested in.

Taking factor Beta seriously, we can damn the torpedoes and order full speed ahead on the vital life of the ingroup. For those who gather around the Lord's Table, tasting of a common cup, also must share a common life, at least at the depths where experience matters. If a church is a church at all, it is a fellowship of the faithful who sense some very strong common ties. To this end, some simple suggestions are in order.

No association is meaningful until there is a high level of motivation in common. The principal complaint in this volume is that the visible church of today is nearly fatally diluted by numbers of those who don't care enough. The answer proposed is to emphasize the rather considerable power of those few who are highly motivated, rather than to try and pump the whole mass up to an operational level. So with fellowship:

the strategy could rightly be to conduct a program in which the inner core is invited into a discipline of relating, thereby challenging the others to care more.

Although earlier in this writing some critical glances were cast in the direction of adult study groups, we take up the cry here in another wise. The intimacy of small numbers being together cannot be surpassed; if one Christian knows and trusts two others, and finds sublime dimensions to this friendship at the Communion table and in worldly witness, there is the church. Notice the two dimensions of that sentence—a small-circle atmosphere of acceptance and a relation of the circle *in toto* to the church. It might be better said that we are advocating churches within the church, yet being careful not to fragment the church.

The temptation here is to dissolve into programmatic innovations, graphs, charts, and parish organizations as a method of building an answer. This approach simply won't do; it assumes that everyone's need is similar and his response predictable. The church is a living organism, and as such, grows rightly as does organic life. The basic unit is the "cell," which is made up of a nucleus, other surrounding incomplete particles of life, all suspended in protoplasm. Each cell not only lives by interaction with other organic material, but also brings other cells into existence by the simple reproductory expedient of dividing itself in half.

Using factor Beta, those who were too limited in interest to be involved in Christian growth could be left alone on the innocuous level of premembership. Those who are willing to be confirmed in ministry become parts of living cells, circles of six to ten who meet for prayer and mutual ministry. These cells would have a stipulated life span (six to ten months), after which they would divide in half, receive new members, and proceed. The purpose of these groups is principally to effect reconciliation with the church, for it will be frankly recognized that every person is offended by the judgment of the gospel and needs healing. Within these circles will be honesty and the enhancing of the individual. Where such experiences may be damaging (as they can be), the process of reconciliation and the expression of forgiveness will be all the more the task of the next such cell. These circles might conceivably become so meaningful as to be the units in which persons come to the Lord's Table together (as members of orders in coming to Mass).

Throughout the whole system must be considerable elasticity, freedom, yet a commonly held discipline. Some individuals come equipped with enough innate security and wholesomeness of self-acceptance as to absorb the assurances of such a group and never need it again, exuding the warmth of Christian fellowship in all pursuits. Others face any relationship with such hesitation that honest involvement may take months. Some would become quickly dependent upon a group, and use it as a covert from any outside storm, others would intuitively become manipulators and improvisors. Thus the central authority in any congregation, such as the session, would have to keep pastoral contact with all involved, and stand ready and trained to guide with love the development of each person's interpersonal pilgrimage.

It is strange that in the face of overwhelming evidence, the church continues to make fellowship an accidental side issue in its offerings to the world. Claiming to be the successor to the healing touch of the apostolic family, the church yet stood by to watch Alcoholics Anonymous pierce the vacuum within the heavy drinker's heart. This wouldn't be an apt illustration if there had been a professional discovery involved, but AA is really an association of amateurs sharing a common problem in concern. It stole the church's thunder without the church ever missing it; we went serenely and traditionally on through the ceremonial gyrations of the centuries, wondering why the world didn't storm our gates to find the answers.

The office of pastor is not yet obsolete; in fact, its value could come up several notches to the glory of God. Someone, somewhere, has to carry the symbolic nature of the church; in Christianity, with its respect for incarnation, that symbol is always a *person*. A pastor is primarily, and above all, a person—a mortal and fallible *man* (or woman) who is thoroughly involved in the conflicts and paradoxes of being human and having faith. After that, he is the living characteristic of the church, representing its *intent* in all that he does. When he visits the sick, it is the whole church making the call, expressing its concern, offering its prayers. When he presides at a marriage or a funeral, it is the whole congregation who is there, performing the ministry, sacramentalizing its love. When he preaches the gospel, he is the ear of the church pointed toward God and the mouth interpreting what is heard, and the man who assumes personal responsibility for the consequences of the Word.

But a pastor is only validly a pastor when he rightly represents the pastorate of that congregation. He is only so when he is a pastor among pastors. Unless that which he symbolizes is actual, he is not even yet a pastor himself. Unless, for instance, there is a fellowship of real concern in the congregation, the pastor only represents himself, and therefore he is not a pastor but just a concerned Christian. The call on the sick is only one man showing that he cares. Of course, this is important, even happily commendable, but no different from any visit from any person. However, if he is "sent" by the spirit of a fellowship to whom human suffering is a burden, and intercessory prayer a flavor of life, then his visit brings the whole splendor of "fellowship" to the bedside.

Unfortunately, the space-time limitation upon humans means that the pastor cannot really have a one-to-one relationship of any depth with all his flock. It is the wise pastor who knows this, and is quite deliberate in choosing his circle of intense associations. Within this circle he is no more than a man who needs to experience God's acceptance from his fellow Christians; from this circle, leadership is given to the other circles. Thus the pastor is, indeed, personally involved as all Christians must be, but not spread so thinly around the congregation that everybody's friend becomes nobody's friend. In a sense that all the leadership then become pastors, the professional leader is at his best as a *primus inter pares,* a catalyst who stimulates that atmosphere of acceptance which brings fellowship, yet is not either the author or the essence of the fellowship. Here, of course, is where the advantage of a charismatic personality is to be seen. True leadership is the setting of a pace, the challenge of a standard, the invitation to emulate, that enthuses the membership to enhance their own dignity by supporting. Where there is a pastor who trusts and accepts people, there can be fellowship. Where a pastor can't be this way, it may well be his copastors, the lay leadership of the congregation, who can.

A further element to be considered is the internal image of the church. Undoubtedly, a strong contributory cause to the early church's intensive inner loyalties was what we would now call the minority complex. It was the sense of isolation, even alienation, from a hostile and unregenerate world, that bound the early Christians to one another in a resolution of support and evangelistic fervor. As long as official or majority disapproval prevailed, the church sharpened its ministry within. But now that beautiful and venerable buildings dot the landscape of modern cities, houses of worship that are acknowledged by Christian and pagan alike, and there is no visible organized resistance to the church, there seems little need to huddle together to salve the no longer existing wounds of martyrdom. It was only a generation ago that the church still felt an oppressive inferiority heaviness upon it as it saw the world so jollily successful at its sinning, and the inner image became that of harboring the real truth about righteousness, and it was slightly bitter that the world seemed so all-fired disinterested. Distorted as it was, it contributed to a sense of mutual purpose that made more of a fellowship out of the Wednesday night prayer meetings than most after-service coffee times ever get to be now.

It would be most improper to suggest that the church ought to get on a paranoid binge as a method of firing up its spirit of fellowship. It would be wrong, because it is both neurotic (like Hitler's making ritualistic victims of the Jews) and unnecessary. The church only has to review its doctrines of church and world to see that a real cleavage, far more profound than the obvious persecutions of Roman times, yet exists. In a way, the world is still picking on the church, but in these times it is happening so subtly that we lose the sense of difference. Inasmuch as the church calls men to repentance, it must see with careful accuracy how the world devalues and resists the concept of human failure before God. As the church calls all men to their highest privilege of submitting to the glory and wonder of obeying God, it has to see that we live in a world that prefers idolatry, especially the idolatry of clever, amoral man. As the church offers men the reconciliation it has found in Christ, it dwells in the midst of a people to whom reconciliation is as much of a threat as it is a blessing. All the antagonisms, the hostilities, the rejections of the world that drove the early church into underground assemblies of faith, commitment, and love, are still our stubborn contemporaries. That we are not so dismayed by them as to seek one another's solace in facing them to the glory of God shows more the blindness of the church than the blandness of the world.

It is the vision and message of the church, accurately assessing the truth about gospel and world, that originates the fellowship. A church whose teaching has no element of crisis has no reason to band together in purpose. Even worse, a church that fails to identify the real target of the gospel develops into an association of those who have written in their own less worthy goals, as seen in an earlier chapter. This message is not just what the pastor says in the pulpit. Individual congregations can be characterized by the consensus of the real message as seen in their corporate life, the goals of their giving, their impact on the community, the handling of people, and the dealing with problems.

A study of what we call the ecumenical movement will show that we are trying to accomplish corporately what we have imperfectly found locally. The sense of urgency for unity has arisen with strength and persuasion, not from the central life of the institutional church but from its cutting edge. The cry for cooperation and the hunger for mutual respect have come from the mission fields, and the firing line where church and world clarify their mutual criticisms. Protected by programs and habits of centuries, the old-line parts of the church were content to proceed with denominational identities and traditional doctrinal hairsplitting. It was "out there" where Christianity was interpreting itself to the primitive, the ancient non-Christian culture, the garbage-strewn streets of the inner city, the disgruntled minority, and the power structures of the political world, that the idea of a common witness made sense. Not only do the divisions make the message incomplete, even ludicrous, but those who are the evangels sense a deep longing for one another. There is a wry twist to church history in the fact that the World Council of Churches, now lauded by the official leaderships, had to be promoted so largely from without. The symbol of layman John R. Mott, first honorary president, seeking the longed-for reality of unity in the Protestant fold that had spawned his beloved Y.M.C.A., is apt. It is quite apparent that when the church looks at itself it sees many reasons for purity by specialization which result in fragmentation; when it looks at the world, it closes ranks for mission.

So the conciliar movement, which has now ripened into warm conversations and gestures of respect between Rome and the rest of us, is a most genuine indication that the Holy Spirit has not forgotten us. And in like manner, it is evidence that our basic unspoken purpose is indeed to win the world for Christ. Denominationally speaking, we are becoming more willing to give up the dignity of being the "more correct" ones to the reality of needing one another to fulfill the integrity of the church. The Roman Catholic Church has pretty well been able to function through the years as a self-contained unit, and could conceivably do so for quite a while to come. Yet upon the ascendancy to the Holy See of John XXIII, it took only a suggestion from his lips to unlock evidences of a vast and long-lasting hunger on the part of thousands in that communion for world Christianity to acknowledge its belongingness. We need one another, and the sense of shame that we have stayed apart for so long is heavy upon us. The writer is no ecumaniac who thinks that the Heavenly City will be lowered from above when we're all under one denominational roof, but he does make bold to say that when we can acknowledge the diversity of the church with pride and gratitude, we can also acknowledge "greater works than these" that can be effected by the Lord of the church, and our hope is greater.

Ecumenicism is Christian fellowship in macrocosm. The development of meaningful interpersonal relationships in any given congregation is ecumenicity in microcosm. They are two parts of the same whole and will bless the church by occurring in concert. He who can work in respect with his brother whom he hath seen will be ready to deal with the disciplines of witness within a larger scope that he cannot readily see. Thus true Christian fellowship is the human side of the basic high doctrine of the church as the body of Christ, with members of different function, but belonging to the same body. The church will rise to the unbelievable demands of the twentieth century when it is composed of those whose concept of the church is extraparochial, and whose sense of personal responsibility is elastic.

A valuable lesson is found in glancing at the intramural conflicts of Christian history. Both in the great schisms of the past and in the denominational and congregational divisions of the present the factor that led to disgrace and tragedy was the unwillingness to face the reality of conflict. "Rather," said the erstwhile sages repeatedly, "go our separate ways than retain fellowship when we can't agree; we musn't conduct undignified warfare among ourselves." No one will probably ever be able to catalog the divisive groups, churches, denominations, and movements that have been the result of strong differences, whether doctrinal or psychological, and from which all parties have fled to have their own way privately. Nobly, but rarely, have there been examples of that kind of maturity in the church in which conflict is recognized as a constructive, though painful, stage.

Interpersonal collisions need not be seen as always disastrous. The Holy Scriptures resound, from Abraham and Lot through to Peter and Paul, with honest illustrations of petty bickerings and hurt egos. This seems to be an unavoidable fact of life, and as such it needs to be accepted and used. Just as murder is completely unacceptable as a method of solving any social problem, so should the breaking of fellowship in the church be equally heinous when the inevitable misunderstandings arise. Although it is always more difficult to endure a problem until solution and reconciliation evolve, yet the superior requirements of churchmanship make it mandatory. No one person, or group, or theological flavor, has the right to rupture the divine body, no matter how righteous he may think his cause. And no aggrieved individual has the right to divide, or even leave, the church on his own, over a difference of personal opinion, no matter how deeply he may feel about it. The integrity of the church is more important than the fragile egos, or even worthy causes, by which we are all affected.

This means to point out that the church is, when its ministry is meeting humanity rightly, a battlefield in which the term "Christian fellowship" embraces the tolerance of conflict, the free expression of ideas, and the framework in which those of strongly different attitudes can yet feel related and accepted. This is far easier to achieve on the larger scenes of church activity; it is at its most excruciatingly delicate within the local congregation. Where the level of concern for truth and purity is high, there also will be an intensity of emotions that can too easily be the seed ground of conflict. So be it. Let the matter be faced, and the conflict acknowledged within the fellowship, and let the church speak, depending upon the wisdom of the Holy Spirit. And when it has thus spoken, let those who differ show their real allegiance to the Lord of the church by participating in it with zeal to his glory. It can be done, it has been done, it is being done, in exemplary fashion among those whose leadership is most effective, and it can be the identifying mark of vitality within the church.

It is under the subject of Christian fellowship that a discussion of intercessory prayer and the miracle of healing is most relevant. These were the characteristics of apostolic times; they have always been dramatically present at the threshold of the Golden Ages of the church, and they are as appropriate to the twentieth century as they have been to all the others. Intercession is the collective act of a body of those who care. The Christian church was born into a world of savage primitive hostility, in which respect always went to the powerful, and the innocent were victims of a strange and apathetic fate. That part of Christian life that few could understand was a love, expressed at any cost, for the unlovable, and a concern for the lost world. From the beginning, the church felt its purpose most clearly when it interceded before God for the very world that had rejected Christ, but for which he had yet died. The pulsating activity of life, which has been the mark of the church at its best, has ever since been that of praying, and working, and giving, for others.

Intercessory prayer is as natural to the church as breathing is to any man. It is the church's privilege to be involved in the sufferings of others, and when this cannot be manifested in works of mercy or words of assurance, it takes the wings of prayer. True to the promises of the New Testament, this type of prayer is the bringer of healing. Perhaps most obvious is the healing of the church itself. Just as any community bands together when someone suffers a tragedy, surrounding that person with the ministry of concern, forgetting its own less important problems, so is the church healed of its cracks and fissions, its paltry disgruntlements and hesitancies, when it shows its true concern for others. The history of the missionary movement, from the famous haystack prayer meeting of 1808 to New Delhi in 1962, has been marked with the healing of countless insignificant wounds.

But the second healing that is of the concern of the church is also a promise fulfilled. Admittedly, the theology of intercessory prayer is most confusing because it goes crosscurrent to several other remarkably respectable theological premises. Yet, it is not for the church to demand rationality in its own most profound experience, but to pursue the expression of care on all fronts. It happens to be a matter of historical fact, known more by intuition and faith than by statistical research, that prayer effects healing. My own experience of knowing beyond question the upholding strength of those who prayed for me at an especially trying time is sufficient evidence for me; I only wish that the thousands who are suffering in solitude could be known and directly prayed for.

The *koinōnia*, the beloved fellowship, cares about its members; its real validity is found in its care for the world outside. Its prayers of supplication are for itself as an instrument of the Holy Spirit; its prayers of intercession are for the world it has been sent to rescue for Christ. John Donne stood before the literates of history, not as a poet or a sage, but as a Christian of all centuries, in his classic stanza, "No man is an *Iland* . . ." We do, indeed, belong to one another, and every living man is our burden.

NOTES

1. Paul S. Minear, *Images of the Church in the New Testament* (The Westminster Press, 1960), pp. 55–56.

2. *Ibid.*, p. 15.

3. Quoted by James B. Ashbrook in an article, "The Church as a Matriarchy," in *Pastoral Psychology* (Sept., 1963), p. 44.

4. Ernest C. Moore, *The Story of Instruction* (The Macmillan Company, 1938), p. 86.

5. Philip Schaff, *History of the Christian Church* (Charles Scribner's Sons, 1922), Vol. II, p. 256.

6. Hans Lietzmann, *A History of the Early Church* (Meridian Books, Inc., 1961), Vol. II, p. 131.

7. MacKinley Helm, *After Pentecost* (Harper & Brothers, 1936), p. 323.

8. Moore, *op. cit.*, p. 88.

9. Dom Gregory Dix, *The Shape of the Liturgy* (The Dacre Press, Glasgow, 1954), p. 41.

10. *Ibid.*, p. 391.

11. *Ibid.*

12. John T. McNeill, *A History of the Cure of Souls* (Harper & Brothers, 1951), p. 89.

13. Dix, *op. cit.*, p. 437.

14. *Ibid.*

15. *Ibid.*, p. 443.

16. Kenneth Latourette, *A History of Christianity* (Harper & Brothers, 1953), p. 217.

17. *Ibid.*, p. 1464.

18. George H. Williams, *The Radical Reformation* (The Westminster Press, 1962), pp. 447–449.

19. *Ibid.*, p. 449.

20. *Ibid.*, p. 451.

21. Quoted by Ralph Sockman, *Protestantism, a Symposium* (Parthenon Press, 1944), p. 206.

22. I found this little jewel in a century-old book by Charles Hodge, *The Constitutional History of the Presbyterian Church,* published by the Presbyterian Board of Publications in 1851. Hodge is unknowingly struggling with factor Beta and can't quite identify the problem area.

23. Donald Anderson McGavran, *How Churches Grow* (World Dominion Press, London, 1959), p. 58.

24. Geddes MacGregor, *The Coming Reformation* (The Westminster Press, 1960), pp. 72–73.

25. J. B. Pratt, *The Religious Consciousness* (The Macmillan Company, 1943), p. 123.

26. Wayne E. Oates, *The Christian Pastor* (The Westminster Press, 1952), p. 16.

27. Blanche Carrier, *Free to Grow* (Harper & Brothers, 1951), p. 162.

28. Pratt, *op. cit.,* p. 127.

29. Ian D. Suttie, *The Origins of Love and Hate* (The Julian Press, Inc., 1952), pp. 142–143.

30. Albert E. Day, *An Autobiography of Prayer* (Harper & Brothers, 1952), pp. 23–24.

31. Harold Begbie, *Twice Born Men* (Hodder & Stoughton, Ltd., London, 1909), pp. 30 ff.

32. Paul Johnson, *Psychology of Pastoral Care* (Abingdon Press, 1953), p. 116.

33. This can be found in two words of the remarkable Dr. Boisen: *The Exploration of the Inner World* (Harper Torchbook, Harper & Brothers, 1961) and his wonderful autobiography, *Out of the Depths* (Harper & Brothers, 1960), pp. 121 ff.

34. Boisen, *The Exploration of the Inner World,* p. 79.

35. Lewis Sherrill, *The Gift of Power* (The Macmillan Company, 1955), p. 124.

36. *Ibid.*

37. R. G. Collingwood, *Religion and Philosophy* (Macmillan & Co., Ltd., London, 1916), p. 9.

38. *Ibid.,* Sec. II, Ch. 2, *passim.*

39. Basil A. Yeaxlee, *Religion and the Growing Mind* (The Seabury Press, Inc., 1952), pp. 123 ff.

40. Reinhold Niebuhr, *An Interpretation of Christian Ethics* (Meridian Books, Inc., 1956), pp. 18–19.

41. *Ibid.,* a chapter heading.

42. James Luther Adams, *Handbook of Christian Theology* (Meridian Books, Inc., 1961), p. 139.

43. Dietrich Bonhoeffer, *Ethics* (The Macmillan Company, 1955), p. 18.

44. Niebuhr, *op. cit.*, p. 23.
45. *Ibid.*, p. 24.
46. Bonhoeffer, *op. cit.*, pp. 43–44.
47. Niebuhr, *op. cit.*, p. 154.
48. Bonhoeffer, *op. cit.*, p. 174.
49. *Ibid.*, p. 265.
50. *Ibid.*, p. 74.